A Sportsman's Life

A Sportsman's Life

How I Built Orvis by Mixing Business and Sport

Leigh Perkins

with Geoffrey Norman

Atlantic Monthly Press
New York

Published simultaneously in Canada
Printed in the United States of America

FIRST EDITION

Library of Congress Cataloging-in-Publication Data

Perkins, Leigh.
    A sportsman's life / by Leigh Perkins with Geoffrey Norman.
    p. cm.
    ISBN 0-87113-757-7
    1. Perkins, Leigh.   2. Businessmen—United States Biography.
3. Fishing tackle industry—United States—History.   4. Orvis
Company—History.   5. Fly fishing—Equipment and supplies.
I. Norman, Geoffrey.   II. Title.
HD9489.T332P476   1999
338.7'68879124'092—dc21   99-26364
[B]

Design by Laura Hammond Hough

Atlantic Monthly Press
841 Broadway
New York, NY 10003

99 00 01 02   10 9 8 7 6 5 4 3 2 1

To my wife Romi and my children Perk, David, Molly, and Melissa, who have tolerated and, to a great degree, enjoyed my sporting life. They are my favorite companions.

Acknowledgments

I had a lot of luck and a lot of help building Orvis. I'll thank Mom and Dad for the luck, I was born lucky, but there are several people who, while they are not mentioned in the text, were crucial to the success of the Orvis company or made my job easier and more fun. I would like to take this opportunity to recognize and thank Lisa Chitham, Dick Davis, Ann Dupree, Stephanie Jacob, Jim Lepage, Jim Logan, Evelyn Madis, Judy Maier, Gloria Merrow, Leigh Oliva, Tom Rosenbauer, Everly St. Peter, the late Anne Secour, Mary Sprague, Lea Talcott, Dotty Thompson, Laura Towslee, Lori Vilbrin, Cheryl Wilcox, Pat Workman, and Joan Young.

I would also like to thank my friends in the world of conservation, whose work has insured the survival of the sporting life in America. There are many of them—too many to single out by name—but I would like to express my gratitude here and also by donating my share of the proceeds of this book to The Nature Conservancy.

LHP
Manchester, Vermont
May 1999

Introduction

A few years ago, *The Wall Street Journal* sent a reporter up to Vermont to talk to me. I assumed he wanted to ask me about how my company, Orvis, had become one of the leaders in the direct-mail industry, and it was certainly a story I liked telling. We are all proud of our successes.

But the reporter seemed almost as interested in the way I spent my time outside the office as he was in my contributions to the success of the Orvis company and the way I ran my business. He seemed especially interested in the fact that one of the legendary trout streams of the eastern United States—the Battenkill—flowed through my backyard in Vermont and that during the spring and summer you could often find me there, with a fly rod. And that I spent three or four weeks every winter at my plantation in northern Florida for quail and duck hunting. And that I fished for bonefish and tarpon in the Florida Keys in the spring and also traveled to Argentina, New Zealand, England, Africa, and a lot of other places for the sport.

It seemed perfectly logical to me. Orvis sold more than tweed jackets and fishing rods. It sold a way of life, and it made sense to me that the boss was living that life. But when we totaled up the places I'd gone and the number of days that I'd spent in the previous year hunting and fishing, I had to admit that my life sounded fairly enviable.

"Well," I said to the reporter, "you can say this for me. I never gave anyone a reason to feel sorry for me."

I was just making a wisecrack. Trying to give a reporter a good quote for his story. But now that I think about it, that doesn't seem like a bad way to approach your life. Don't feel sorry for yourself, and don't give anyone else any reason to feel sorry for you, either. I've tried, and I've done a pretty good job. I think I can say that I succeeded in business. When I bought the Orvis company in 1965, I paid $400,000 for it—$200,000 in cash and $200,000 borrowed against inventory. In 1996, the company grossed more than $200 million. So my company was a success, and I'm proud of that. I also managed to do a lot of what many men like to do most in this life, which is go hunting and fishing. And because that's what my business was, I could call it work. Not a bad deal, if you can get it.

I worked hard, of course. When I bought Orvis, the mail-order business was in its infancy. Orvis had been sending out catalogs since 1856—longer than anyone in the United States—but in 1965 direct mail was still less than half of the Orvis company's business and a tiny segment of the retail industry. This was before the days of easy credit-card ordering over the telephone, before we started using computers to analyze customer lists and follow inventory. What little bit of business was done through catalogs consisted of orders that came in by mail and were paid for by check. Those were the dark ages, even before Fed Ex and UPS. Goods were shipped by U.S. mail.

So I found myself getting into a fledgling industry when it was right on the verge of a period of explosive expansion. I had to stay on top of things just to keep up with the innovations, much less the growth, and I think I contributed both to the industry's new ways of doing things and to my own company's success. That meant paying attention not just to the changing needs of anglers and bird hunters, but to the dynamic situation in the mail-order industry as well.

The recreation and leisure fields began growing enormously just after I bought Orvis, and they haven't slowed down since. Our company had to stretch to keep up with the demands of an expanding market, and that meant we had to work; but I found it interesting and even fun, so I never thought of it as hard.

Orvis was in a fluid industry with lots of new products and aggressive companies, and if you didn't innovate and stay ahead of the curve, then you quickly got left behind, which is what happened to a lot of my competitors from the early years. My own goal was to produce the very best fly-fishing and bird-hunting products possible, because I believe that quality equipment enhances the quality of the experience on the stream or in the field. I was young and it was exciting. I can honestly say that I never got up dreading going to the office—and that's where I was really lucky.

I'd been one of those boys who would rather hunt and fish and just be outdoors than anything, even though I played sports and got interested in girls when I got old enough for that. But I was always in love with the outdoors. When I was a teenager, I wanted to be a trapper or a naturalist. My mother, who appraised my talents a little differently, thought I'd make a good dog trainer. I should say here that my mother taught me a lot about hunting and fishing. When I was growing up, I was her companion on a number of fishing trips; I'll get into that a little more later on. But it is fair to say that when she said she thought I'd make a good dog trainer, that wasn't a negative judgment in any way. She had a lot more respect for dog trainers than she did for most businessmen.

I never lost my feeling for the outdoors or my love for hunting and fishing. In my whole life, I have missed only two weekends of hunting during bird season, once because I had polio and once to get married. I feel the same thrill I've always felt when I cast to a tailing bonefish on a flat or to a rising cutthroat on a spring creek. I love the whistling sound of ducks passing low overhead in the marsh before sunrise. I still love to watch a pair of dogs working a field of broom sage, and a covey rise of quail still blows my mind. I was fortunate to have found something I loved so much when I was young, and even more fortunate to have been able to stay with it after I was grown. And most fortunate of all, maybe, in being able to turn that passion into my livelihood.

I never had to worry about taking time off to do what I really wanted to do, because I didn't think in terms of vacations and time off. I never felt guilty when I was off shooting ducks or fishing for tarpon and never felt like I should have been back in the office, going through the paperwork. I was always interested in new ideas for the business because they might mean more success in the field, and I always wanted to know what my fishing partners had to tell me because it might just turn into a new product for the catalog. I didn't have any trouble believing in what I was selling because I used Orvis products when I did the things I most liked to do. They had to be good because I was my own most demanding customer.

Unlike a lot of sportsmen, I didn't resent it when new people came along and got interested in hunting or fishing. I didn't see novices crowding the streams; I saw, instead, new customers who were learning the sport and would soon be pushing for better fish and wildlife conservation, which meant better fishing and hunting for the future. Over the years, some of those customers became friends and companions. If a sportsman likes the rod you sell him, then he might very easily become your friend. Because of this, I've met people and made friends all over the world. I've done some fishing with Jimmy Carter and some fishing and shooting with Ted Turner, among others. It's hard for me to say exactly where the business starts and where it becomes the sport.

Which is just another way of saying that nobody has any reason to feel sorry for me.

Chapter 1

In My Mother's Footsteps

When I bought the Orvis company, I was thirty-seven years old. I was the third owner in the company's history. It was my third job.

I didn't really need a job, since I'd been born into a wealthy family. My grandmother was a niece of Mark Hanna, who had worked his way up from the position of ship's chandler to become a very successful industrialist whose business was based on coal and iron mining and Great Lakes shipping. So I suppose I inherited a gene for business.

But I could have passed up a business career and done something else less demanding. I don't remember that I was ever tempted to do that, even though I certainly enjoy my time playing. But the question is worth thinking about. People will say, about me or somebody like me, "Oh, he had it made. It's not like he started with nothing. He was rich from the beginning."

Now, there is something to that. But there are two sides to the story, especially when you are talking about entrepreneurship. If you already have some money, it can be very easy to say, "The hell with it. I don't need this," and walk away when you run into a rough patch in business—as you surely will. I've seen it happen. In some ways, starting out with money makes it easier to fail. And it certainly makes it easier never to try and, especially, never to try seriously.

I've learned—mostly from other people's examples—that if you don't try seriously, that if you approach your business like a dilettante, then you will inevitably fail. You may not care whether the business is growing or not. But the key people who are working for you care intensely. My own son, when he was a senior in college and full of the kind of ideas they put into you there, asked me why the company had to keep growing. "Why can't we just stay the same size," he asked me, " and keep doing what we know how to do and are good at?" At the time, I explained the facts of business life to him, and he seems to have taken them to heart. Since he took over as CEO in 1992, the Orvis company has kept right on growing, doubling in size and tripling profits, and having some of its best years ever.

I would never say that being born into a wealthy family was a liability. But I will say it was no guarantee I would succeed with Orvis. Which, by the way, I bought with money I had made in my second job, not with money I'd inherited.

While I could have become some kind of playboy—going in for golf or tennis or polo instead of wing shooting and fly-fishing—I chose to work. I was greatly influenced in this decision by my father, who didn't give me a lot of advice, but when he did, it was always sound. He told me that he knew only a few men who did not work and were happy and that they were inevitably men of very high intelligence. He added that he didn't think I qualified, and I didn't argue with him.

It seems almost inevitable, in hindsight, that I would wind up not just in the business I got into, but owning the exact company that I bought and ran for almost thirty years. Orvis and I were a natural fit.

Fishing and hunting and the outdoor life are in my blood the way they are for so many American men—and, these days, many women as well. I had grown up caring passionately and intensely about those things, the way other boys cared about cars or sports. I just couldn't get enough.

While that made me a pretty typical American boy, there was one way in which I was unusual if not downright unique. Most boys learn about fishing and hunting from their fathers. The great influence in my sporting life was my mother. She taught me to fish and hunt, and she was my principal sporting companion for the first eighteen years of my life. It was an unusual situation, but it had a lot of advantages, especially in the disciplinary department. As my brothers and sisters often pointed out, I could get away with just about anything.

My mother was an attractive woman and a fine, competitive athlete. She was evidently born with a love for fishing and hunting in spite of the fact that neither her father nor her mother hunted or fished. She was, fortunately, born in Thomasville, Georgia, which is the capital of quail hunting in America. She was one of the finest wing shots I have ever known, easily better than I ever became. Nash Buckingham, who wrote wonderfully about outdoor subjects, especially bird hunting, once wrote about her this way:

> In Mrs. Perkins I saw a quail shot at work who needn't ask odds off any quail shot, man or woman. [She] not only knows the techniques of quail gunning, but of the bird itself, the dogs, and the shots. . . . I never saw her out of position; she was invariably on time at the post, shot quietly and decisively. In short, she was the finished product. . . . In the woods, after singles, I several times saw her wheel and bring down wild flushing quail. They were the type of shots many hunters pass up for fear of missing. But she took 'em as they came.

When a covey of quail flushed, my mother routinely got a bird with each barrel of her 20-gauge Winchester 21, and there is a picture somewhere in one of the family scrapbooks of her mounting the gun as a covey is rising. Somebody wrote a caption to that photograph that reads, "Katherine gets her customary double." It was no exaggeration.

I was riding along in the shooting buggy with her from the time I was one year old and not long after that went along in the punt boat while she hunted alligators. One of my early memories is sharing a boat with a twelve-foot gator that she had just shot. Gators do not stop moving for several hours after they have been killed, and the experience left quite an impression on a three-year-old boy.

I wasn't much of a student. From an early age, my mind was on the outdoors instead of the books, and, as it turned out, I had what would be called today a learning disability—dyslexia. Mother had never bothered with higher education herself and didn't consider my time away from the books at all wasted. As I said, she thought I might grow up to become a good dog trainer and handler.

When we weren't down south, hunting quail and alligators on the family place near Thomasville, we lived on a farm outside of Cleveland where we raised corn, oats, wheat, and timothy and where the other kids in the family rode horses. There were six of us children all together. We used to say that we were two litters. Dad had three with his first wife, who died, and then there were the three of us who were his children with my mother. I was the only one who wasn't into horses, because I had violent hay fever.

I made up for it with other things, especially fishing on a nearby pond that was owned by a neighbor who gave me the run of the place. It was a paradise for a young kid, and I would ride my bike over there and spend the day exploring and catching bluegill, pumpkinseed, and bass. I taught myself a lot about the fundamentals of fishing on that pond. I learned how to make a careful approach, which most young people don't have the patience to do, and which I am still convinced is more important than just about anything else in fishing. You can easily scare a fish if you blunder in on it, making a lot of noise or showing a big, conspicuous profile. They are wild, wary creatures, and that is especially true of some of the greatest game fish—trout and bonefish, for example, which you tend to find in clear, shallow water, making them even more alert and more of a challenge.

So I learned how to make a careful approach when I was getting in range to make my cast. Then I learned you have to make an accurate cast—or "presentation"—and that you have to use the

right bait or lure and change when what you're using isn't working, even if it was right the day before. Later on, the expert fly fishermen I got to know would talk about this and say the fish were
being "selective," and you had to observe the fish and experiment
until you found the right fly.

I was interested in more than just the fish on that pond. I
caught turtles, too, and I got some pretty painful bites when I
grabbed them by the wrong end. I caught bullfrogs with a red fly
that I tied on to a cane pole. I caught salamanders and the occasional snake. In the evenings, after a day on the pond, I would come
home with a stringer of bluegills and a couple of bass hanging from
the handlebars of my bicycle.

Those were glorious days, and, like most dedicated anglers, I
remained determined that they would never end, even when I went
on to other places.

My love of the outdoors was pretty much the dominant theme
in my life even then, and by the time I was eleven, I had been kicked
out of the Hawken School in Cleveland for regularly playing hooky
to go fishing in the nearby creek. My father was the disciplinarian
in the family—the only thing my mother could think of to punish
me was to keep me from going on fishing trips with her, but that
meant denying herself a companion. So Dad enrolled me in what
was supposed to be a tough boarding school called Forman in Connecticut. It turned out to be a good solution, and I certainly didn't
mind since the boys at the school lived in tents.

There was a nice little stream not far from the school where
I could sneak off and catch yellow perch and bullheads and another
stream where I refined my angling skills on brook trout. I've never
needed a lot of sleep, so I would slip out of the tent early in the
morning and head off for the creeks. I also ran a trapline but didn't
catch much except for the occasional rabbit. When this happened,
I would take one of my pals down to the stream in the middle of
the night, and we would cook the rabbit over a campfire.

I wasn't content with the occasional rabbit, however, and my
enthusiasm for the outdoor life got the better of me and got me into

a little trouble. When we went to soccer practice, we were driven six miles to the field in the back of a pickup truck. When I spotted a roadkill skunk on the way to the field, I would "accidentally" lose my cap. Then, on the return trip, I would get the driver to stop so I could pick up the cap . . . as well as the skunk. Skunks brought a pretty good price in the fur market back then, and I would skin out my prizes down in the locker-shower room.

The second time I pulled that stunt, the night watchman noticed the odor. The school had just hired some Korean kitchen help, and this old entrenched Yankee workman, who didn't take to foreigners in the first place, was sure they were causing the stink in the kitchen, which was located just over the locker room. So he woke up the headmaster at about 1:30 in the morning. The headmaster was a little more perceptive than the night watchman, and it didn't take him long to discover me in the act of skinning out a skunk. The next morning at breakfast, the scent from my good work was evident to all, and word got around pretty fast who was behind it. The headmaster wasn't a bad guy, and I'm still impressed that he managed to keep a straight face when he caught me—literally red-handed—with that skunk.

All in all, the Forman School was a good experience, and I worked a little harder at my studies than I had before. The school reported to my father that I might make a reasonably productive citizen (nobody said anything about my becoming a dog trainer) but that college was probably out of the question. So Dad decided that it was time for me to move on to a more challenging school. I said good-bye to my little Connecticut streams and moved on to the Asheville School in North Carolina.

Asheville was a good school for me. I learned even more discipline under the two best teachers I ever had. Wilbur Peck taught math the old-fashioned way but made it interesting, and math was always my best subject. And Bill Hutchins, whose brother was the famous president of the University of Chicago, Robert Maynard Hutchins, taught me English with the kind of patience and encouragement that made it possible for me to overcome my dyslexia and learn to enjoy reading and communicating. I owe a lot to both men.

But I didn't neglect my main interests in life while I was at Asheville. Although I played football and soccer, I managed to get assigned to a one-boy bridge-building detail with no supervision around Lake Ashnoca one year, instead of doing sports. This provided opportunities for some good bass, bluegill, and crappie fishing. I also managed to run a trapline and take a few muskrats. On one occasion, my mother and father came down to the school for a visit, and Dad stopped as they were crossing the grounds, pointed to a room, and said it was mine. When Mother said, "How can you tell?" he said, "How many other kids would have muskrat hides hanging out of the window?"

The best part of my continuing education in the outdoors during those Asheville years took place in the summers when I went on fishing trips up into Canada with my mother. Between my freshman and sophomore years, we went on my first Atlantic salmon trip, to the Madeleine River on the north shore of the Gaspé Peninsula. We reached the camp by a long hike on a woods trail and slept in tents right on the river, which we could hear flowing past us in the dark. There was no refrigeration, so we dammed a little feeder stream to make a pool where we could keep whatever salmon we caught alive until it was time to go back. We had two pools on the river where we fished. One was right in front of the camp, and the other was about seventy-five yards upstream. It was a wild, remote river, and there were plenty of salmon in it, making their way back upstream to spawn. The Atlantic salmon is sought after by the most dedicated and capable anglers in the world, some of whom believe that all other kinds of fishing are second rate. I don't feel that strongly, but it was a memorable experience to be on that river, fishing for those fish. I would climb trees and look down into the pools and watch them holding there so I could tell my mother where to place her fly.

We were using the finest tackle that was available in those days: bamboo rods, silk lines, and gut leaders. It would all be considered hopelessly obsolete and primitive today. You had to be good to make it work, and even then, it was tough. Those were strong fish. Mother was still learning, and I was an absolute novice. The first few salmon that we managed to hook all broke off. But there was something so powerful and magnificent in the way those strong silver fish ran and jumped that we didn't mind at first. Then we got a little bit desperate, since we wanted fish to eat. We finally managed to catch some, and I think it was probably then that I graduated from bass and bluegill to the great game fish that I have spent so much of the rest of my life fishing for all over the world. I still make at least one Atlantic salmon trip every year, and like a lot of anglers I've made financial contributions and worked with other anglers to try to restore the salmon to their previous numbers.

My mother and I made other trips for salmon while I was at the Asheville School, and we both got better and came to love the fishing more and more. We went to the legendary rivers in New Brunswick, the Restigouche and the Upsalquitch, and while salmon fishing was pretty much a man's sport back then, Mother's reputation as a sports lady—especially as a wing shot—had preceded her, so she got on to some of the best water at the best times of the season. Since I was her fishing buddy, I got to go with her.

She was not much for the fixed routine of the camps, which called for a leisurely breakfast followed by a morning of fishing, then lunch and a little rest period, followed by some more fishing and then dinner. This schedule was considered sacrosanct, but Mother didn't care. She would get a guide to take her out early, and often she would catch a fish before breakfast. Soon everybody else in camp started following her example. The guides didn't much appreciate it, but it was a lesson to me. You take advantage of opportunities, especially when they are as rare and special as being on one of the world's great salmon rivers.

When I was sixteen, on one of those trips to the Restigouche, I was using a sixteen-foot, two-handed rod made by Leonard (one of the Orvis company's strongest competitors in those days) and casting a big fly—a number 2 Green Highlander. I got a take from a very large salmon, and to this day I can see that fish coming out of the water with its hooked lower jaw wide open and its thick silver body hanging over the river. I managed to hold on and land the fish, which turned out to weigh thirty pounds, a trophy salmon on any river. It was the thrill of my young life, and I think my mother took more pride in that fish than I did. I have never caught a larger salmon.

I wasn't neglecting the hunting side of things during those years. I spent Christmas and spring vacations at the family plantation, Spring Hill, near Thomasville. The plantations, like the one that belonged to my parents, had come into existence in the late nineteenth century when wealthy families from the North—especially Cleveland and New York—would go south in the winter looking for some relief from the cold. The last stop on that train line was Thomasville, where there was a luxury hotel.

Life in Thomasville was chiefly social, with parties and such, which bored a lot of the men, who began asking the locals if there wasn't something to do around those parts in the way of sport. They said that there was pretty good bird hunting, which turned out to be true. So the northern families began buying up land in the area—which was cheap since the boll weevil had led to a cotton crash—and soon there were these large holdings of several thousand acres complete with antebellum-style plantation houses, servants, dog handlers, and other staff all devoted to quail hunting.

The style of hunting that developed was this: The hunters would sit in a wagon that was pulled through the open pine woods by mules, while a dog handler worked English pointers from horseback. When the dogs found birds, the wagon driver would whoa the mules, and the shooters would get down and move in for the covey rise.

There is nothing else quite like a covey of bobwhite quail bursting out of the broom sage for pure drama and excitement. The birds seem to explode from the grass in one tight mass that is really nothing but a blur, and then they separate and fly hard, angling away from the hunters through the pines, each bird a little brown shape that seems to be moving faster than you could believe possible. The challenge is to keep your poise and not try to shoot into the whole mass of birds—you'll always miss—but to pick one, follow it, and make your shot. If you hit that bird and are quick enough and composed enough, you still have time to pick out another and get off another shot before the birds are all out of range.

When we hunted, I rode the wagon, shot birds, and helped work with the dogs (my mother still had hopes for me in this regard). I also hunted turkeys, which were still plentiful in those parts but had disappeared from much of the rest of their natural range. I went into the little cypress swamps and hunted ducks, and I also shot doves. I looked forward to Christmas, if it was possible, more than any kid at school. By now, I was utterly hooked. Hunting and fishing were the keenest pleasures in my life.

But I was also still a schoolboy, and with the help of those good teachers at Asheville and the influence of my father, a loyal and devoted alum, I managed to get accepted by Williams College in the Berkshire mountains of Massachusetts. I was fortunate—as I've often been—in getting the opportunity that Williams provided. I got a good education and, not surprisingly, found plenty of opportunities for fishing and hunting while I was there. I also made my first direct contact with the Orvis company while I was at Williams, and that may have been the luckiest break of all.

I discovered that there was good hunting around Williams for grouse and woodcock. But you couldn't hunt in Massachusetts on Sunday, so I began going across the state line, into Vermont, with my classmate Pete Finlay. He lived in Dorset, Vermont, where there were plenty of good grouse and woodcock covers. I had a very good bird dog named Leda, and we had a lot of success. On the way to Dorset, we would drive through Manchester, Vermont, which was the home of Orvis and the famous Battenkill River. On our way through one day, we stopped, and I bought my first Orvis rod. It was an eight-foot, three-piece, impregnated bamboo rod for an HDH line, and it was my absolute pride and joy. I used that rod for many, many years. It was made by a man named Wes Jordan, who was one of the big names in fly-fishing back then, and who later became one of my employees.

There were a lot of people making bamboo rods back then, and most of them were of very uneven quality. Even a rod maker with a big name would turn out bamboo rods that were junk. The grading was unreliable unless the rods were handmade by one of the great makers. Wes Jordan had developed techniques that insured that his factory turned out rods of reliable quality. In fact, anglers back then believed that the rods he produced for Orvis were better than the individual handmade rods of the famous makers like Payne and Leonard, who were thought by a lot of anglers, including me, to never make any two rods the same. An Orvis rod was something you could depend on, a fine angling piece, which you took a lot of pride in owning.

The day I bought that rod, I thought about how great it would be to work for Orvis and be associated with people like Wes Jordan who were masters of the sporting world. The thought occurred to me every time I went past the store on my way to my grouse and woodcock covers up in Dorset or to fish the Battenkill River.

But any idle thoughts I had about a career at Orvis—or anywhere else—were just that: idle thoughts. I was working hard (for me, anyway) at school, and when I wasn't studying or going to class, I was doing the other things that interested me most in life. In other words, I was fishing or hunting or driving here and there, meeting girls.

Maybe because of my experiences on fishing trips with my mother, I thought I could combine girls and fishing. One day, I took a pretty girl to the Deerfield River, which had some pretty good fishing in those days. I had a rod for her but no waders. That didn't seem to be a problem since the river was low. But I saw some rising fish across the river in a deep hole and decided we had to get over there and try for them. So I put my date on my shoulders and tried to carry her across the river. Naturally, I tripped about halfway across and submerged my date, which put an end to that romance and my thoughts of combining girls and fishing.

Still, I had some success in that department. By the beginning of my senior year, I was engaged to a girl I had met through my sister. Mary Hammerly was a student at Connecticut College, where I was driving on the weekends when I wasn't up in Vermont, hunting birds.

On one of those bird-hunting weekends, I woke up with a blinding headache. But it was Sunday morning, so I put it down to the effects of Saturday night and put on my boots. By the time I had shot my first bird and should have been feeling better, I was worse. Much worse. I kept at it and shot another grouse, but I was feeling so bad I couldn't even go after it to pick it up. I had to sit down. After an hour or so, I could not stand up, so I crawled back to my car on my hands and knees. I was barely able to drive back to school, where I went to the infirmary and was diagnosed with polio.

Back then, in the days of the terrible polio epidemics, when you got the disease, you became a ward of the state. I was sent to a polio hospital in Pittsfield and put in a ward full of people who were a lot worse off than I was. Many of them were in iron lungs.

I was there for three weeks. But my incredible luck held. I lost twenty pounds and had some severe headaches but no other symptoms and no paralysis at all. Mary and my roommate Doug Garfield both visited me regularly. My father also visited. My mother was on a grouse-hunting trip in Michigan and did not visit. I understood that entirely.

I missed a lot of school and was worried about the comprehensive exams that I had to pass in order to graduate. I'm not usually a worrier, but to this day I have nightmares about not being able to find the room where the exams were being held and of being totally unprepared.

Doug Garfield was also behind but not because of polio. He had led a very active social life, and we both had to study like hell that spring to make it out of Williams. But we both passed, and after graduation, on a fine Saturday in June of 1950, I got married. My bird dog, Leda, had just had a litter of eight Brittany pups, and I gave one to each of my hunting ushers. Mary and I honeymooned in France, then went on to Switzerland and Scotland, where we fished for trout. Mary knew what she was in for and decided to learn to fish and hunt.

When we got back to the States, I got my first real job and started raising a family. For the next twelve years, Orvis was merely a pleasant memory and the name on my favorite fly rod.

Chapter 2

Working in the Mines

I knew I was going to work, then, when I finished my education. But I wasn't sure what I'd be doing or where I'd be doing it.

As it turned out, my first full-time job was in the mines, the iron mines of northern Minnesota, as an employee of the Hanna Mining Company. I had a lot to learn and a lot to prove. I was fresh out of Williams College, with a new wife and a baby on the way. I had asked the president of the company for a job—which was something I could do because he was a neighbor—but there was nothing make-work about the job, and I certainly didn't start at the top. As a matter of fact, I started pretty much at the bottom. But jobs weren't easy to get in 1950, so it didn't bother me that even though I was a recent college graduate, on the first day of work I was the rod man on a survey crew. It was real no-brainer work, but I was glad to be working. I wasn't in some kind of executive training program. They didn't have anything like that, so I suppose I could have stayed out in the field until I retired. But I never thought it would work out like that.

Mining is hard, serious, dangerous work. It didn't make any difference to the people in Minnesota where I had gone to school or what family I came from. They wanted to know if I could do the job. I started as an engineer's helper, and after a few months, I was promoted to pit foreman. The way it worked was that you took some ore from here and some from there until you got the right mix for the grade you wanted. Pit foreman was a good job, but you didn't win any popularity contests if you did it right. You had to make sure your crew was making its production quota of so many loads of a certain grade ore, every shift, and you couldn't necessarily be nice about it. But you couldn't just be a hard-ass, either. You had to know when to push and when to back off. And these were the kinds of things they didn't teach you in college.

I worked either the afternoon shift—three to eleven—or the night shift—eleven to seven—six days a week. The day-shift foreman was the man with the big responsibility. He set it up for the rest of us.

One day, I had a crew out somewhere, and they were slow doing whatever it was that needed to be done. So I kept them there until almost quitting time and then drove them back in the bed of a pickup. I drove a little fast and bounced them around pretty good. They were mad about it, and they waged a slowdown the next night at work.

The day foreman was a very tough, very capable little Italian guy named Russo who knew one hundred times as much as I did, even though he hadn't had one tenth of the education. He was also a total authority figure. Everybody respected him, and everybody listened to him.

Well, when he learned what was going on, he pulled me aside and said, "You screwed up. You had a situation, and you handled it badly. If you've got a problem with these people, you tell them about it and work it out. Now, I'll fix it for you this time. But I'm not going to bail you out again; you're going to have to take care of your own problems." Then he talked to the boys in the crew and said, "This guy's just a kid. Give him a break." After that, things went pretty well, and I remember the miners as being a bunch of good guys who treated a kid from Cleveland who had a silver spoon sticking out of his mouth damn decently.

I learned a big lesson from that episode and from working around Russo. What I learned was how to get along with all kinds of people. That was as important as anything I've learned in my entire life. And I learned to respect the foreman on any job, the guy who makes the thing actually work. In a plant or a machine shop or just about any business, you have the people who design the system and you have the people who actually work with it on the factory floor and who know how to tweak things and jury-rig them to make them go.

This is one of the reasons I haven't got a lot of good things to say about the people coming out of MBA programs. They almost always have a very superior notion of their own abilities and importance and tend to look down on the kind of person I'm talking about, the foreman who knows how to make things run. But when you get into trouble, the MBAs don't have the hands-on experience and the common sense to make the fixes. I forgot this once, much later, with Orvis, and it damned near cost me the company.

I picked up some other skills that came in handy. When we had a strike, and the supervisory people were still coming in to work with nothing to do, I got the master mechanic to teach me how to weld. At the time, I used those skills to make myself a boat trailer and a couple of sets of fireplace tools. A little later on, I used them to get my foot in the door at another company and move my career along.

I honestly enjoyed working in the mines—the way you enjoy any job if you throw yourself into it. It felt good to be working in the real world after all the years I had spent in school, studying abstract things that didn't seem to have any practical value. Compared to some of my subjects in school, meeting production schedules seemed like an eminently real-world skill. So I worked hard, did well, and got promoted from pit foreman to foreman at the sintering plant. There was more responsibility there since it was a dangerous place where the fine ore was baked with coke, forming a sinter and making it ready for the blast furnaces. Safety was the foreman's primary responsibility, and there was nothing routine about it. Before I got there, a sampler—whose job was to go from one railroad car to the next, taking ore samples—had been jumping from one ore car to the next to save time, instead of climbing down from and then back up into each car. It is the kind of shortcut people will always take if you let them get away with it. This man had fallen into an empty car just before it was filled with a load of hot sinter.

That kind of thing will get your attention, and I took the work seriously.

One night, a sampler working on my shift showed up for work drunk. He was an ex-con, and he didn't like it when I sent him home. It may have been the day's pay as much as the insult, I don't know, but when I thought he was gone, he came up from behind and took a shot at me with a railroad brake iron. He was so tight, though, that his aim was off, and he just grazed me. We started fighting, with the other miners just watching to see how it would turn out. He was about my size and pretty drunk, so I was able to whip him. The word got around, and that helped my reputation.

About six months later, I was about to be transferred to Hibbing—which was the big town in those parts—and some of the miners threw a party for me at the local bar. Things turned stupidly melodramatic when the ex-con I'd had the brawl with walked in. Everybody went quiet and waited to see how it would turn out. I walked up to the man and held out my hand. Fortunately, he took it—he was sober and probably could have done a lot better this time if he'd wanted to fight. We shook, and he said I'd done the right thing. Like most of the miners, he wasn't a bad guy.

While I was learning a lot in Minnesota that would eventually help me in business later on, I wasn't exactly neglecting the sporting side of life. Because I was working the night and afternoon shifts, I had all day to hunt or fish. I was young and didn't need that much sleep, especially since Minnesota has some of the best ruffed grouse hunting anywhere in the country. The local guys were mostly deer hunters, so I had the grouse hunting pretty much to myself. I've never been much for big game hunting. I like bird hunting, primarily because of the dogs, and I was still hunting with my Brittany, Leda, one of the best dogs I have ever owned. We had some fine days together in the cutover aspen thickets.

I bought a second car when I went to work for the mines. It was a '31 Chevy, and I picked it up for fifty-five bucks. I called the car Old Lizzy, and it was mostly for hunting. I figured that when people saw it out on some country road they would just assume it had been abandoned. I didn't want anyone figuring out where my best grouse-hunting spots were.

Later on, when I'd gotten to know some of the crew, they played a little trick on me. When I took off a week for vacation, they gave Old Lizzy a face lift. When I came home, she was painted canary yellow and had baby blue fenders. There was no mistaking her when I was parked near one of my favorite grouse coverts.

One last thing about that car. I sold it at a profit. Got seventy-five dollars for her, three and a half years after I bought her. I've never done that well with cars since.

I also hunted ducks in Minnesota—ringneck (still one of my favorites), bluebills, and redheads. In the spring and summer, I fished for crappie, walleye, and bass in the lakes and caught small brook trout in some of the brushy little streams.

All in all, it was a fine life, and I was enjoying myself enormously.

If there was a downside, it was that the mining country of Minnesota was not the ideal place to raise a family. Living conditions could be harsh. Before I started in the mines, I went up ahead, to pick out our first house. It was nothing more than a converted two-car garage. The rent was $20 a month. I believe I was making about $450 a month at the time. But it was pretty austere: linoleum over concrete, kerosene heaters. The kerosene froze when it got down to forty below—which it did, every now and then. Sometimes I would come into that house, tracking snow, and it would not melt. After the baby came, my wife found more suitable quarters. A two-story house with three bedrooms and bathrooms upstairs and down. Real luxury at $45 a month.

By the time our second son was born, we had been in Minnesota for five years and were starting to think about another place to raise the family. We had gone to a wedding in Detroit, and my wife was especially charmed by the fact that the men and the women stayed in the same room at parties and talked to each other.

In Minnesota, the women would all stay out in the kitchen, and the men would find another room in the house where they could talk.

At the end of 1954 I quit the mines and started looking for something new. I had learned a lot, and I'd had a lot of fun. I didn't know, for sure, what was next. But I was looking forward to it. With any luck, it would be as much of an adventure as Minnesota and the mines had been.

Chapter 3

Birth of a Salesman

Before I made my next career move, my wife and I did something that made a deep impression on me and probably influenced a lot of what I did with the Orvis company later. We went on a trip to Cuba, as the guest of a friend on his parents' large yacht. We started on the southern coast and cruised down to the Isle of Pines. The water in this area was a lot like that in Florida Bay, with miles and miles of shallow flats where you could find bonefish and small tarpon.

While I was an avid angler back then, I had never fished much in salt water. I had brought along a seven-foot, nine-inch Shakespeare/Howell Wonder Rod for a six-weight line. It was one of the first fiberglass fly rods ever made and a gift from my brother Stub. It was designed and developed by Doc Howell, who was a partner of my brother's in a small company that made parts for the electronics industry. The other people on our trip to Cuba used plug casting equipment, which was generally too heavy for bonefish. And the tarpon were able to throw the plugs almost as soon as they were hooked up. So, always being eager to try new things, I used the fly rod and was very successful.

Bonefish are one of the wariest of all game fish. You find them on shallow flats in clear water, and if you put a line over them or throw a heavy lure or bait too close, they will spook and tear off the flat into deeper water. A lot of the challenge of bonefishing is in stalking the fish, getting close, and then making a long, delicate, accurate cast without scaring the fish. With that fiberglass fly rod, I could put a fly down in front of a bonefish so softly that I didn't spook him, and, even though the rod was a little bit light for the job, I could sink the hook when a tarpon struck. So I did better than anyone, with tackle that was considered much too delicate for salt water fishing back then.

I didn't realize it, but during that time there were anglers up in Florida Bay who were pioneering the whole world of salt water fly-fishing that would become such an important part of the sporting scene—and my business—in years to come. One of those pioneers was Joe Brooks, who was one of America's greatest fly-fishing anglers and whom I met later, during the Orvis years. To this day, one of the things I enjoy most in life is poling across a shallow flat in a skiff, looking for bonefish, permit, or tarpon. These days, however, I use a graphite rod that is made by Orvis.

When I got back to the States after that trip to Cuba, I actually worked with my brother at the plastics company for a brief time. But he lost out in a corporate power struggle, and I left with him. I wasn't there long enough that I even considered it a real job.

But it was not very long before I was back at work, this time with a company that made gas welding and cutting equipment, called Harris Calorific, on the west side of Cleveland, the city where I had grown up. Once again, I didn't exactly start at the top. For the first few months, I was doing piecework on a drill press, which meant that I didn't get to demonstrate the welding skills I'd learned during that strike back in Minnesota. But they definitely came in handy later, when I moved into sales.

Starting out, though, I wore an apron and goggles, and I worked on the floor. I punched a time clock, like the rest of the machine tool operators. This lasted for a few months; then I got moved up to purchasing agent. I kept pushing to get into sales. Even though we were a manufacturing outfit, I thought sales was the heart and soul of the company because talking to customers and figuring out their needs was what drove the decisions about what we produced. When I was hired, I knew that there was going to be an opening fairly soon at the top, and I thought I had a chance at running the company. But first I had to get into sales, and after a while, I got my wish.

My territory covered about one fourth of the city of Cleveland. It was 1956, and I made $100 a month (which included expenses) and got a 20 percent commission on my sales. Good salesmen did okay at Harris, and the bad ones didn't cost much as long as they stayed, which wasn't very long. I was determined to do well and last.

I have always been aggressive, and, like a lot of people who are that way, I thought selling came down to finding likely customers and then making your pitch. I found out fairly quickly that it isn't that easy.

I was going around to the factories and the junkyards, knocking on doors and demonstrating our equipment. I gave a good demonstration and was getting plenty of them, so, at first, I thought I was doing okay since the sales manager evaluated us by the number of demonstrations we made during a week. The problem was I wasn't closing many sales. I spent a lot of time explaining the advantages of Harris torches and giving flame-cutting demonstrations and generally showing potential customers how wonderful our equipment was, but they weren't buying. And in sales, not surprisingly, you are *truly* measured by how much you sell, no matter how much attention your sales manager pays to demonstrations. Getting your foot in the door is better than getting it slammed in your face, but you still have to close the deal once you've gotten inside.

I was getting pretty discouraged and was actually desperate enough to try something I didn't really believe in. But I hoped it might just work. I signed up for the Dale Carnegie course.

The courses were at night, after the working day was over. I had a good-looking wife and three sons at home as well as lots of friends, and there were things I would have much rather been doing at night. But I went to the classes, just the same, expecting a lot of warmed-over common-sense stuff. But by the time I finished, my thinking had changed entirely. I learned a lot about selling from Dale Carnegie, and I still have a lot of respect for that program.

The most important thing I learned from Dale Carnegie is that a good salesman is, first of all, a good listener. You have to find out what your customer is interested in—what he really wants—before you can sell him anything. And the way you learn is by listening to what he has to say.

So instead of just going around giving my pitch and demonstrating our equipment, I started asking people questions. If I could show that our equipment would cut costs, I'd ask, would that influence them to buy? Or, if I could show that it would increase production, would that convince them? I listened, and when I found out what it was they were interested in, I would do a demonstration to prove that our torches would cut costs or increase production—depending on what I'd learned about their needs. And, if I couldn't get a commitment, then I wouldn't give a demonstration, since it wouldn't accomplish anything except to inflate a number that pleased the sales manager but didn't improve my bottom line.

My demonstrations went down by about half. But my sales resulting from those demonstrations went from about 15 percent to 70 percent, and my commissions went up about 400 percent, from about $150 a week to $700.

It seems like such a simple lesson, but a lot of the really important things you learn about business are simple. And I've never stopped listening. Right up until I retired, in 1992, I worked the phones at Orvis now and then—and I insisted that just before Christmas, all the company officers and top-salaried employees take a shift on the order phones. I believed it was important for all our staff to know who our customers were and what they were thinking.

Taking catalog orders from customers might not sound like the best possible use of the CEO's time. But I find that listening to customers talking on the phone, even when they think they are talking to an order taker, is a good way to learn what they think about your company and your products. You learn what they like about you and, maybe more important, what they don't like. For instance, someone will say, "Now, this jacket isn't going to leak, is it? I got one just like it from another company, and it started leaking the first time I put it on." Right away, you know that there might be a problem with the jackets, and you make sure that yours don't leak. And that people know that if they do, they can get a refund, no questions asked. Questions that people ask on the phone, for example, help you realize what you didn't explain very well in the catalog copy. I don't think there was a time when I spent two hours on the phone when I didn't get an idea about how to make either the product or the catalog copy we used to describe it work better.

As my success as a salesman at Harris Calorific grew, so did my responsibilities in the company. It wasn't my plan to be a salesman all my life—I wanted to run the company. It was the reason I was working in the first place, and why I was working hard and doing things like going to Dale Carnegie night courses.

By 1958, I was vice president of sales at Harris Calorific, and things were going pretty well. The company was thriving. I had a staff of sixteen people working for me, and I was riding pretty high. But 1958 was a bad year for the economy. The country was going into a serious recession. The president of the company was a man named Tony Taylor. Everyone called him Tough Tony, and he'd earned the name fair and square. He saw problems coming for the industry and the company and decided we needed to cut back to be ready. He wanted to trim our payroll, so he called me in and said that he wanted me to cut eight people from my department. I went back to the office and thought about it and came up with what I thought were some great reasons we shouldn't make those cuts. I had the figures to back up my case for how well we were doing— our sales were increasing in spite of the recession—and why we didn't need to let those people go.

The next day, I went into Tough Tony's office, full of confidence, and I made my pitch for why I needed each and every man in my department. I told him I thought we were on the verge of even bigger things, and when I finished, I felt pretty confident that Tony would see it my way.

He'd listened to my little speech without interrupting, and when it was his turn, he simply said, "Perkins, if you haven't got eight people cut out of your payroll by the end of the week, then I will do the cutting myself, and you'll be one of those eight people."

I went back and let eight people go. We made it through the recession in good shape, and I learned that the time to cut is before you start losing money, not after.

I should mention one other lesson I learned while I was at Harris Calorific. This one came early in my career there, before I even got into sales, but it has been important to me ever since. I noticed that when I was on the drill press or screw machine, doing piecework, that if I had been doing quite a bit of drinking over the weekend, then my piecework production dropped fairly seriously— 20 to 30 percent—on Monday. The falloff was more serious, more like 50 to 80 percent, when I got into sales. To this day, I don't have a beer or a drink with lunch.

That isn't to say I didn't enjoy life while I was with Harris Calorific. I worked hard, but I didn't neglect the sporting life. Since I couldn't just take off someplace for some great fishing or hunting and call it work, the way I was able to do later with Orvis, I had to find the sport nearby and do it after—or before—working hours. When something is important enough to you, then you have to find a way around or over the obstacles. In other words, you have to be resourceful. When it comes to sport, I've always been resourceful.

The city of Cleveland sits on the banks of Lake Erie, which has always been known as great duck-hunting territory. Some of the oldest, most exclusive duck-hunting clubs in the country are located near there.

One day, when I was tromping around in the woods with my two older sons, I ran into a man who would turn out to be one of the great, unforgettable characters in my life. His name was Fritz Neubauer, and he was a true outdoorsman who really understood hunting, fishing, and trapping and lived the life. He'd fought with the Marines in the Pacific, at Iwo Jima, and was pretty well shot up, so he had some income from disability. He made an additional living from trapping until the fur market went to hell. He was a hard-drinking, hell-raising guy with the brains and the wit to get away with some of his behavior. He lived off the land and knew more about marsh management for wildlife than anyone I knew. He wrote stories about it and was a pretty good writer. Once he was on television, debating Cleveland Amory of the Friends of Animals about trapping, and to show that leg-hold traps weren't cruel Fritz set a steel trap and put his hand in it to spring it. Then he said to Amory, "See, this doesn't really hurt them. It just *holds* them." That brought a lot of the audience around.

Later on, I said to him, "Fritz, what do you mean it doesn't hurt?"

"Oh, it hurt like hell," he said. "But I wasn't going to let that son-of-a-bitch know."

My good friend Dick Whitney and I arranged with Fritz to develop a duck club. Fritz leased and managed the land and did a great job of improving it. Dick and I recruited members. We started with twenty members and charged two hundred dollars. Unlike the old, traditional clubs around Cleveland, we allowed women members. Actually, we encouraged them. Neither of us was willing to handle the objections of our wives and our friends' wives if we kept women out, and both of us were progressive guys who liked the idea of having women around. Also, a lot of the women members were not as keen on the duck hunting as Dick and I were, so they weren't showing up very often. Almost all of the members were working types and didn't have any time off except for Saturday mornings. (Hunting on Sundays wasn't legal in Ohio.) But the hard core—especially Dick and me—would be out in the marsh most mornings. I'd drive out there wearing my work clothes—complete with white shirt, suit, and tie. I'd put my waders and my parka on over my good clothes and step out into the marsh in the early morning, before dawn.

On a good morning, the ducks—mallards, teal, wood duck, and Canada geese—would fly, and I would call and shoot for forty-five minutes. Then I'd leave and strip off my waders and parka—just like James Bond, who wore a tuxedo under his wet suit in a movie of the time. I'd arrive at the office, with my clothes only slightly rumpled, ready for work at 8:00. I didn't spend a lot of time during the day wishing I were out in the field, since I'd already been there. On those days when I'd shot well—maybe even taken a limit—I'd be ready to take on the world.

There were days when I wasn't in Cleveland, of course. Like a lot of salesmen, I spent plenty of time on the road. But even then, I wasn't giving anyone a reason to feel sorry for me. Some of the best sport I had was when I was out working my territory. When I was made vice president of sales, I made sure I kept the western provinces of Canada—Manitoba, Saskatchewan, and Alberta—under my direct supervision. The business potential out there was only fair, but the duck hunting and prairie bird hunting were just spectacular. I might have been trying to work my way to the top very aggressively, but I never lost sight of my priorities.

When working my Canadian territory, I would meet with my distributor and his salesmen on Sunday for product reviews and sales approaches. The salesmen didn't like it much, but there was no hunting in Canada on Sunday, so it was the perfect day to conduct that kind of business. I would either get out there early and hunt on Friday and Saturday or stay late and hunt Monday and Tuesday. We hunted ducks—mallards, pintail, and wigeon—in the prairie potholes and sharptail grouse in the big, cutover wheat fields. There was just endless country for hunting, and the game was truly abundant.

The hunting was so extraordinary there that I would come home and tell my friends about it in glowing terms. Finally, after hearing all those stories, Doug Garfield, my old college roommate, decided to come out with me and see for himself. In the fall of 1962 we took a week off from work and went out there for what we considered the ideal trip. It turned out to be exactly that.

We started in Winnipeg, where we rented a car. Then we drove west, hunting across Manitoba and Saskatchewan and ending up in Alberta. We had my dog, a Brittany spaniel named Pepper, with us. The dog pointed the sharptail and huns in the prairies, and we had wonderful shooting. One day, we found a great place for duck hunting, but we needed a boat to get to where the ducks were flying. We'd brought a lot of gear with us, but there was no way we could have checked a boat with our luggage.

Then we ran into another hunter who had a boat and decoys and who'd done so well with the canvasbacks that he was ready to quit and try some bird hunting. We had the makings of a deal. We traded him the use of Pepper for a day, in return for the use of his boat and his decoys. We had good duck hunting, and Pepper found a lot of sharptails for our friend, so it was a good trade, even though I'd say the duck hunter got the better of it. Most sportsmen would a lot rather trust a stranger with their boat than their bird dog. But we were all happy and confident that the trade wasn't risky. That was the way it was out there. The people were some of the friendliest and most generous I've ever run across. There was a lot of sportsmanship to go along with the sport. This is one of the best features of the sporting life—the people you meet.

We made our way west, like we'd planned, hunting in the morning and the evening, traveling during the middle of the day, and camping somewhere—usually around an old, abandoned farmhouse—at night, where we would make ourselves a dinner of sharptail grouse or duck. At breakfast and lunch we ate duck gizzards, hearts, and livers. Every meal was a feast. After two or three days of this, we'd spend a night at a little hotel. For five dollars, we could get a hot shower and sleep between some clean sheets. We stopped once at a hotel in Saskatchewan and found out the place was full. The bartender invited us to stay out at his house. He said his wife wouldn't mind, which seemed like a stretch, considering the way Doug and I looked—and, probably, smelled. But we took him up on it, and, just like he said, his wife was very pleasant and friendly.

They wouldn't accept any payment. It was one of those acts of generosity that you never forget.

Later in the trip, Doug and I were driving down one of the long, empty roads when we saw a covey of sharptail fly and then land in a field with some good holding cover. There was absolutely nothing around us anywhere. No sign of civilization. Not a house for fifty miles and certainly not a town. So, even though it was Sunday, we decided to put Pepper out for a little work. Anyway, we rationalized, we were out of game, and we needed a couple of grouse for supper that night. So we loaded our shotguns and followed Pepper out into the field. We were breaking the law, but it was hard to see how anyone would ever know.

We got our birds for supper and drove on. When we came to a little town, Doug wanted to stop and check on the World Series game. Then, when we were driving out of town, an official-looking vehicle, painted olive green, pulled us over. It was the game warden. He asked to see our licenses, to check our guns, and—here is where it got dicey—to look inside our trunk. We'd heard that a game-law violation could result in the confiscation of your gun and your car, so this was pretty serious business. I don't think either of us felt very good about violating the game law in the first place, and we felt even worse about it with the warden standing there while we opened the trunk for his inspection.

The grouse we'd shot were there. He looked at them and asked for an explanation.

"Oh, *those* birds," we said. "We shot those birds yesterday."

He looked at me and said, "Well, then, why do you still have blood on your hands?"

I wasn't ready to give up. At that point, I figured, the best defense was a good offense. So I got all indignant, and I stuck my finger in his chest and said to him, "Look here, mister, don't you get personal with me. My washing habits are my business, not yours."

Doug was standing behind the warden clutching his sides and trying to keep from laughing out loud.

The warden was young and easily intimidated. He apologized and asked if he could take a couple of wing samples off the birds for a survey. It seemed like a good time to be diplomatic and accommodating.

"Of course," I said.

When he cut the wings, blood spurted out. I think he saw through us then but was too rattled to pursue it. So he took the wings and went on his way.

That was the last time I ever intentionally violated the game laws.

Doug and I pushed on across Canada, having the time of our lives hunting, camping out, and eating duck livers for breakfast and lunch and grouse breasts for dinner. We were reluctant for it to end, so we spent our last day on a duck marsh in the vicinity of Edmonton, where we had plane reservations. The shooting was just wonderful, and we were determined to get our limits and take the ducks back home with us. Consequently, we finally left the marsh about three hours before our plane took off. We were about two and a half hours from the airport, so Doug drove while I plucked and dressed the ducks in the backseat of our rental car.

If you have never tried to push duck feathers out of the window of a speeding car, let me give you a single word of advice: don't. Pretty soon we had a blizzard of duck feathers circulating around the inside of the car. They were so thick that Doug was having a hard time seeing the road. I was throwing everything out of the window, and the sides of the car looked like the walls of a slaughterhouse by the time we got to the airport and turned it in. We got the dog into a homemade crate and made it to the plane, but just barely. We both had middle seats, and the people on either side of us leaned as far away from us as they possibly could.

When we got home, Doug and I both noticed that we were experiencing a lot of pain in our joints. Especially in our feet. So we visited our respective doctors and got the same unusual diagnosis—gout, caused by the overconsumption of duck innards. The treatment was some kind of medication that almost turned you inside out. But it was worth it.

It had been a great trip, the kind you talk about for a long time afterward, and Doug and I kept saying we were going back to do it again. But we never did.

I suppose some seeds were planted in my brain about the possibilities and the excitement of traveling for sport. The trip certainly made an impression in every other way. Later, in the Orvis years, I traveled a lot more, to more exotic destinations, because I knew that my customers wanted to do the same. But I was smart enough to understand that they wanted to do it in style. These days, Orvis endorses lodges where somebody else does the cooking, the food is first rate, and you don't have to worry about giving yourself the gout or plucking birds, or wonder when your next hot shower will be.

Chapter 4

A Company of My Own

I enjoyed being in a supervisory position at Harris. Vice president of sales carried responsibility, and I liked that, but it wasn't enough. I wanted to run a business. I thought I was qualified and that I was the logical choice once Tony Taylor decided to step down. Tony had come out of retirement to run Harris, and it was expected that he wouldn't remain very long.

But Tony had other ideas. He brought his son into the business, and his son soon became president and heir apparent to Tony as CEO. I actually got along fine with his son and thought he was a capable guy. But not as capable as I was.

It became clear that I was not going any higher in that company. I certainly wasn't going to be running it, and since my goal was to run my own company, it was time to make a move.

Equity in Harris Calorific was widely held, and in the time I'd been there, I'd managed to acquire about 14 percent of the stock. The problem in a situation like that is finding a buyer. I was young and impetuous, so I had the bright idea of going to Tony and saying, "What would you take for your stock in Harris? And, if you aren't interested in selling, what would you offer for mine?"

Tony looked at me from across his desk and said, "I'll tell you what, Perkins. I wouldn't give you a dollar a share for your stock, and I wouldn't take a hundred dollars a share for mine. Now what are you going to do?"

That should have closed those doors pretty firmly.

But I didn't know when to quit. So my next plan was to convince the board and the other stockholders that I had the brains, the energy, and the vision, and that I should be the guy to lead the company into the future. I told my friends Dick Whitney and Jim Reid about my plan. Dick was second in command at McGean Chemical, and Jim was heir apparent as CEO of Standard Products, a manufacturer of automobile parts. Their advice was to talk to someone they both listened to, and that was John Drinko.

John was the managing partner in the firm of Baker Hoestetler, which was one of the three top law firms in Cleveland and one of the best in the country. John is not just a smart lawyer; he has brilliant common sense. So much, in fact, that he's now on our board at Orvis. His advice to me then was very simple.

"Give it up," he said when I told him about my plan. "The company is doing well. Tony is the experienced old hand, and you're the kid. The board and stockholders aren't going to be interested in rocking the boat. You'd just be shooting yourself in the foot."

Drinko told me that what I needed to do was get out of Harris and find something of my own. I took his advice, and I'm enormously glad that I did.

I was fortunate enough to find a buyer for my stock, and after eight years with the company, I was out of Harris Calorific with about $400,000. I was thirty-four years old. I had a wife, three sons, and a daughter. I had worked in the mines of Minnesota for five years and in the welding business, selling cutting torches, for eight. I felt I had proved I could do a good day's work in a hard job and that I had what it took to sell. Now I was ready to prove that I could run my own show. I had made enough money in the sale of my Harris stock that I could go out and buy a business on my own hook, not through an inheritance.

What I knew was steel and steel fabrication, and that is where I started looking.

So for almost two full years, I searched for a company to acquire. I dealt with lawyers, investment bankers, and accountants.

John Drinko was my main guide through this new and unfamiliar universe. He had enough confidence for both of us.

I learned a lot from John. He's a West Virginia poor boy by birth who had succeeded hugely in the law and in business. He has a very straight-ahead way of looking at problems and kept me from making the kind of mistakes you are prone to make when you've had a little success and start thinking that you are better and smarter than you really are. I remember one of the things John told me was to avoid buying a company that was losing money on the belief that you're somehow smart enough to come in and turn it around. It was the kind of advice I needed to hear.

So we looked, and I listened to what John Drinko had to say. We investigated several possibilities, including an overhead crane company, a fiberglass replacement auto body parts company, and a pipe wrench company. I found something to like in just about everything we looked at and probably would have gone for one of them if John hadn't said no.

One of my most vivid memories of John and the way he handled things during those negotiations is of a night when we were eating dinner at his country club with the chief financial officer of one of the companies we were looking into. The CFO was exceedingly pompous and high-handed, and at some point during the meal, John just got fed up. He told the man to shut up and eat his dinner and eat every bite since he was paying for it and that when he was finished with his dinner he could go home and wait for us to call.

This was an entirely new approach to business negotiations in my experience. But I liked it—no bullshit, no beating around the bush, just straight ahead, right to the point, all business discussion. I might add that the man cut the crap, ate his dinner, thanked John, and went home quietly.

That is John Drinko's style.

Eventually, an investment banker came to me with a company in Utica, New York. It was called Horrocks-Ibbotson, and it manufactured and packaged low-end fishing tackle, everything from fish hooks to rods. Now, it had never really occurred to me to look for a business that was connected with hunting or fishing, even though that's how I spent just about every spare minute. I just never thought that I might make a living at it.

But when this opportunity came up, I was intrigued. I had plenty of time on my hands, so I went out to Utica to take a look. What I found was a run-down plant and a business that was taking a real beating from foreign competition. I didn't need John Drinko to tell me I wasn't interested in buying Horrocks-Ibbotson. But that visit got me thinking. Thinking about another fishing-tackle company, and one that I had a history with. Orvis, to be exact.

I hadn't thought about Orvis as a business opportunity until I looked at that decaying operation in Utica. But once the thought of buying Orvis got into my mind, I couldn't stop thinking about it. So when I got home from my trip to Horrocks-Ibbotson, I put in a call to Dick Finlay, who was the brother of Pete Finlay, my hunting and fishing mate at Williams. Dick was working at Orvis at the time, so I asked him if he thought there was any chance the company might be for sale. He said he didn't think so and reminded me that the last time I'd done business with Orvis—when I bought my prized rod—my check had bounced. I assured him my check would be good this time, and he suggested that I talk to the owner, Dudley Corkran, who was known to everyone as Duckie.

I called Duckie, and he said the company wasn't for sale but I should come see him anyway. I was trained as a door-knocking salesman, and that was all I needed to hear.

The first meeting went well enough, and I got a picture of what I was dealing with. Duckie pretty much ran the whole show. He had only a few employees, and they all answered directly to him. He was a detail man, to say the least. He was also approaching seventy and getting tired of the personnel problems, which is what happens when you micromanage people. But he and his wife, Skippie, had no children, and he had few other interests. He played golf and he fished for salmon, but the Orvis company was his life, and he was intensely proud of the business and the sense of quality that it represented. I'm certain that he worried about what would happen to the Orvis reputation once he left the business.

From the beginning, negotiating for Orvis with Duckie was more like asking a man for his daughter's hand in marriage than buying his business. The whole process lasted nine months. Duckie would name a figure, and I would meet it, and then he would start saying, "Well, the car is extra, and that chair belongs to me." In every case, I'd go right along, but it would end up with Duckie saying, "Well, let me think about it."

Finally, John Drinko went out to Manchester with me to see if we could move things along. I thought I was a good salesman, but John put on a hell of a show.

We were sitting out on the porch of the distinguished old country club where Duckie played golf. There was a magnificent view of the Green Mountains, and John admired the mountains and talked about how much they reminded him of West Virginia, where he'd grown up. Then he talked about how much he admired Orvis and how much it reminded him of other old, established businesses with great reputations. And—subtly, of course—he talked about how much he admired Duckie and all the wonderful things he had done with the business to keep it going during the war and the tough transitional times. Duckie was delighted by all this, and I think he started coming around to the point of view that with this competent lawyer looking over his shoulder, the kid who wanted to buy his business—namely me—wouldn't screw it up too badly.

Finally, we got down to price, and this time I hesitated. Drinko took me aside and said, "If you don't want it at that price, I do." We made the deal.

For $400,000, I bought the assets of the Orvis company. I paid $200,000 in cash and borrowed $200,000 from the bank against the inventory, so I didn't even have to use the whole nest egg I had established from the sale of Harris Calorific stock. We closed on the first day of 1965. Orvis, where I had dreamed of working while I was a college boy, was now mine.

I should mention something here about the background of the Orvis company and the situation it was in when I bought it.

Orvis began as the C.F. Orvis Company in 1856, selling its goods out of a small stone building next to a resort hotel in Manchester, Vermont, which was then a resort destination for tourists from the big cities, especially New York. Manchester rolled up the sidewalks after October, at least until 1940, when Bromley Mountain opened and started drawing skiers to the area.

Charles Orvis conceived of making mailings to his New York customers, and they liked them so much that they began writing to order by mail. Orvis was sending out catalogs and goods in the mail before the Civil War, which means that it has been in the mail-order business longer than any other American company.

In the early days, Orvis made wooden rods. There was a lot of competition among people making rods back then. Some of these competitors made a very few high-quality rods and sold them at a very high price, while others made a lot of rods of poor or uneven quality and sold them cheaply. Orvis produced a modest number of rods of very good quality, and they were relatively affordable.

At first, the rods were made of various woods, especially lancewood and greenheart—these were solid wood. Then, in the 1870s, bamboo made its first appearance in the United States, and the split cane rod became the most sought-after angling tool. The bamboo was cut into strips, which were tapered according to a formula. Those strips were then glued together to make the rod. The skill of the rod maker was evident in the way the individual strips were milled down and made to fit together and the way the taper performed. Some rods were made in very painstaking fashion by master craftsmen, and their work was recognized then and is collectible today. Good split bamboo rods were like well-made violins, and the craftsmanship that went into them was unmistakable.

Split bamboo was state of the art for almost a century. Today, Orvis still makes some bamboo rods for purists. That rod was one of the foundations of the company—and it got raves, too. One satisfied customer, an army general named Strong, used an Orvis rod to catch the first fish taken on a commercial fly rod in Yellowstone Park in 1876. General Strong was accompanied by the secretary of war, the inspector general of the army, and several other senior officers. In his account of the trip, General Strong sang the praises of his Orvis rod and said the rods carried by other members of the party were clubs in comparison. And there was one famous outdoor writer who tested an Orvis rod in 1880 and wrote it up in *Field & Stream:* "I think this: I have the *best* bamboo rod of its weight—six ounces—in America; yes, in the world."

I couldn't have said it better myself.

Charles Orvis was good in the shop, and he had a fertile mind, which he put to work studying fly reels. They were pretty primitive back then—so primitive, in fact, that a lot of anglers didn't even bother with a reel designed to hold fly line. They just used a bait-casting reel. In 1874, Orvis introduced the first modern fly reel with perforated side plates. Those reduced the weight of the reel and allowed air to flow over the line and decrease the rot and mildew. That became the standard for fly reels and still is. You could pick one up for $2.50 back then; today, Orvis sells a similar but much lighter reel for $225.

Another basis for the early success of the Orvis company was flies. Orvis supplied flies to thousands of anglers and began standardizing patterns in a way that had never been done. This was due to the efforts of Charles Orvis's daughter, Mary. After she learned to tie flies, she took over responsibility for the production of flies for the company in 1876. She had a staff of about half a dozen women working for her, and they produced quality flies in standard patterns, which sold in the store for $1.50 a dozen. She was the first person to name flies according to a pattern. The famous Royal Coachman, for instance, was named by her. Before

then, flies had been described by the material used to tie them—
teal and silver, for instance.

Under Mary's supervision, Orvis eventually produced more
than four hundred patterns. In 1892, she produced a book called
Favorite Flies and Their Histories. It was a big hit and became a
standard text in the angling community. The book went through
nine printings. At the time of her death, in 1914, Mary Orvis Mar-
bury (her married name) was considered one of the most important figures in American angling. We produce a catalog of women's
clothing today under that name.

The company's fortunes declined during World War I and again
with the Great Depression, and by 1939 it had only two employees. The old elegant sporting tradition of willow creels and cedar
canoes had died, and Orvis was about to follow it into the sunset
when Duckie Corkran bought the company from Charles F. Orvis's
heirs in 1939.

World War II came along before he had a chance to do much
to change things. The bamboo that Orvis had stockpiled for rod
making went into ski poles, which the company manufactured for
the mountain troops. After the war, Duckie got the rod building
going again and got the company into light-tackle spin fishing,
which was the new thing and all the rage. He got catalogs out to
build the mail-order side of the business, and he built a new store
in Manchester, which was opened in 1956, the 100th anniversary
of the company.

Nine years later, it was my turn to see what I could do with
this venerable old outfit.

Chapter 5

Old Company, New Tricks

Did I have a plan to make Orvis grow from a half-million-dollar company to a two-hundred-million-dollar company? Lots of people have asked me some variation of that question over the years, and the answer is no, not really.

I believed that it had potential for growth, though not as much as it turned out to have. I did the research, and from what I could discover, no company had ever made much money in the fly rod business or maybe even the fishing rod business in general. Orvis was doing better than most, making a small profit in rod sales. But there was more and more interest in the sporting life—in recreation and leisure—and everybody knew that. My plan for growing the business was to put together a catalog of all the trappings that an upscale outdoorsman country lover needed and desired. Fly-fishing and wing shooting would be the principal, image-building fields.

I don't think I had a clue about some of the forces that would drive our growth over the next thirty years. I didn't have any idea about the coming of the credit card or the computer and how, in combination, they would make the boom in mail order possible. And I'm sure I underestimated the appetite of Americans for high-end sport. But I was in the right place at the right time. Which proves, once again, something that a number of my friends, and both my wives, have said about me—that I am a hell of a lot luckier than I am smart. If you can only be one or the other, I'll take lucky.

I did have a strong hunch about Orvis. And I knew I wanted to use the Orvis fly rod as a symbol. Fly-fishing—and later wing shooting—would be the image around which we would build our business, though we would sell a lot more than fly rods and shotguns. We would sell those things that suggested an affinity for the country or outdoor life. It seemed like a respectable plan. But there were problems getting started. There always are.

The first problem was more amusing than serious. When I closed the deal with Duckie Corkran, part of the agreement was that he would be retained on the payroll at $12,000 per annum—his salary before he sold—for five years. On the first working day of 1965, he came into the office with me and said, "Well, Leigh, where is your desk going to be?"

I said, "Where is your desk?"

I knew where it was, but he pointed to it anyway.

"That," I said, "is going to be my desk."

"Oh," he said. "Then where is my desk going to be?"

"Duckie," I said, "you aren't going to need a desk. Go on home. I'll call you when I need you."

He didn't like it much. But it was the only way. He'd been accustomed to making every decision, and all the staff was used to answering to him. There was no way I could run the company while he was around. We eventually became good friends, and he gave me some good advice over the years. I heard later on that he liked to tell his friends in town that "the damn kid" stole his business from him. But I think he was proud to see the way it grew, and he certainly got over his initial fear that I would run his company into the ground.

My second problem was a little more serious. It was with the rod-making operation that was the heart of the business. There were two problems, actually, the first and more urgent of which was that we could not produce enough rods to fill our orders. The answer, of course, was to increase production, but that was easier said than done.

Demand for Orvis rods was steadily increasing, as the Orvis bamboo fly rod was the best, most dependable rod made. The bamboo used in an Orvis rod had been heat treated to draw off moisture and temper the bamboo. Then, after the strips were glued together, the rod was impregnated with a resin and cured. This unique process made the rod impervious to moisture and kept it from taking a "set," or permanent bend. It also gave Orvis rods a distinctive dark brown, almost mahogany, color. It was a revolutionary process in rod making, and the man who developed it was Wes Jordan, who had been hired by Duckie in 1940. I had inherited Wes as plant manager. Wes was a legend in the fly-fishing world. He made rods for—and was friendly with—some of the stars, like Ted Williams, the great baseball player and angler. But Wes was not really a team player, and he certainly didn't believe in my first rule of business, which is: The customer comes first. Wes had kind of a condescending attitude toward the customer, which I saw quite a bit of when I first got to Orvis. It was an attitude you ran into a lot among people in Vermont. They took a suspicious attitude, bordering on hostile, toward all strangers, even customers. And they didn't really seem all that interested in improving business. The joke was that you could go into a store in Vermont and ask for something and be told, "We don't carry that item. Can't seem to keep it in stock."

I found that there was a lot of truth in that joke.

I remember a day when my mother was coming through Manchester, and she wanted to come to the store to buy some Christmas presents. One of our dour Vermont salesladies was waiting on her, and my mother asked about a pillow with a tennis scene on it. Our saleslady said the pillow was not for sale.

"Of course it's for sale," I said. "Everything in the store is for sale."

The customer is always right, even when you know damn well he is wrong. That's my first commandment. And the customer is certainly always right when she is the boss's mother.

The Orvis salesclerk looked at me and said, "Well, what should I charge for the pillow?"

I pointed at another pillow, pretty much the same, and said, "How much is that one?"

She told me, I think, that it was nineteen dollars, so I said, "Charge her nineteen dollars."

The clerk looked at me and said, "You wouldn't do that to your own mother, would you?"

Later on, I heard that the same clerk had been asked how a certain lady's blouse should be worn. "I wouldn't be caught dead in that thing," the clerk replied. It was one of her last transactions with an Orvis customer, but that's what I was up against. Even so, I hadn't expected it from the legendary Wes Jordan, who came into my office one day to present me with a special rod. It was a beauty. He had measured my hand and sanded the grip down so that my thumb and fingers fit just perfectly. The rod felt so good in my hand that I asked him if it was just the grip or was there something else different about this rod.

"Oh, it's a much better taper than the one we sell," Wes said proudly. "You couldn't buy this rod."

"You mean our customers couldn't buy this rod?" I said. Wes didn't seem to catch the tone of my voice.

"That's right," he said proudly, like it was the right answer.

"Why not?" I said.

"Most of them wouldn't know the difference," Wes said.

Well, I wasn't quite ready to butt heads with Wes Jordan, but I wasn't going to put up with this situation, either. I thought about things for a day or two. Wes was nearing seventy and coming to the end of his career. The company had no retirement plan in those days, but Wes certainly deserved some kind of compensation for all his work. His name was virtually synonymous with Orvis.

So I called him into my office again, a couple of days after he'd given me that special rod.

"Wes, I've got an idea," I said. "Let me know what you think. Let's make a series of Wes Jordan signature rods. They'll be the best rods you can make. Just like that rod you made for me. The rod will give your name the recognition it deserves, and for every one we sell while you're still on the payroll, you'll get 5 percent of its price. For every Wes Jordan rod we sell after you retire, you'll get 10 percent as long as you or your wife, Viola, are alive."

Wes liked the idea quite a bit, and we sold a lot of those rods. A good friend of mine gave one to his wife for a wedding present, and she still fishes with it, from time to time, for sentimental reasons.

Since the bamboo fly rod was our signature product, it was pretty obvious that if we were going to succeed as a business, we at least needed to make as many as we could sell. You didn't need an MBA to figure that one out. And since we were selling only about fifteen hundred rods a year, it didn't seem like an impossible task.

But when I brought the number two man in, when Wes Jordan was on the verge of retirement, and told him I wanted to increase rod production by 50 percent, he gave me a real typical Vermont response. Not "Absolutely, we'll get it done," but "It can't be done." He implied, pretty clearly, that he and his crew were happy making the number of rods they were turning out, and they weren't going to be rushed by anyone, and that included the young, flatlander boss.

I needed to find a new superintendent for the rod shop. After a search, I settled on a man who had worked for GE and seemed to have some experience in supervising manufacturing. We were several hundred rods behind. Our dealers and customers were screaming. We needed to get more rods produced. The first thing my new man did was put in two formal coffee breaks for the crew. The next improvement involved taking three of the top rod makers and putting them to work building a cupola over the front steps of the shop. I asked the superintendent what in the hell he was doing, and he told me that the project was designed to insure the workers' safety. The steps could get icy and someone might slip. This was in July. We needed production a lot more than we needed that cupola. Especially in the middle of the summer.

So I canned that man, and when I went back to the search, I remembered another candidate from the first time around and that my gut feeling had been that he was the right guy. He was a young toolmaker from Maine, and he hadn't had a lot of supervisory experience, which is why I passed on him, in spite of my feeling that he was the sort of quiet, "can-do" person I wanted. His name was Howard Steere. When I called him up, he said he had just been to Orvis the day before to pick up a Wes Jordan rod he'd ordered. I asked him to come back and consider the job I had interviewed him for six months earlier. He did, and he took it. He was the youngest man in the shop, but he was a bright, creative mechanic with a real sense of quality and an ability to get things done. In just a little while, he had the shop turning out more rods and better rods—and at a lower cost. Howard stayed with Orvis for almost thirty years and was a vice president when he retired. He was proof of something I believe I knew but either forgot or was afraid to follow through on—sometimes the best personnel decisions you make have more to do with a gut feeling than what you find in a résumé.

With Howard running things, production was not going to be a problem. At least not because of anything he could control. But one thing he could not control was the supply of raw material, namely bamboo, coming into his shop. If he didn't have it, he couldn't make rods. The solution might seem obvious—buy more bamboo—but it was not that easy. Far from it. In fact, it was so hard that, in trying to solve it, I landed in the clutches of the government, which looked, for a while, like it might try to shut me down and maybe even throw me in jail.

The raw material for rod making was bamboo, but not just any bamboo. It had to be a special kind of bamboo, *Arundinaria amabilis,* to be precise, which is commonly known as Tonkin cane and grows only in southern parts of what was called "Red" China

in those days. And it was illegal for Americans to do business with
that country. Duckie had a large inventory of cane, laid up in
a barn outside of Manchester. More than five years' worth, we
thought. But when we inspected the cane, a lot of it turned out
to be useless. I needed to do something about finding a new supply, or we weren't going to be in the rod-making business much
longer, no matter how many orders we were getting or who was
superintendent.

There was no embargo of China by European countries, so I
made a trip in 1967 and called on some rod manufacturers in France,
Norway, and the British Isles. The Sharpe Rod Company in Scotland was a licensee of the Orvis company, making bamboo rods
under the impregnated bamboo process and paying us a royalty.

The manager, Alan Sharpe, took me salmon fishing on the
River Dee and happily agreed to help us with our bamboo supply
problems. I went on to Norway but didn't locate any usable bamboo there; and then to France, where the Pezon Michelle company
was located in a charming little village where Leonardo da Vinci
had died. Pezon Michelle was a competitor and had no reason to
help Orvis out of its bamboo bind. But to my surprise, André Pezon,
who ran the company, was very helpful, showing me all the ins
and outs of their manufacturing and willing to supply us with
bamboo strips. I made essentially the same deal I'd made in Scotland, buying sawed strips of heat-treated bamboo from them instead of the raw poles from a supplier in China. This was far from
a meaningless distinction, either economically or legally, as I soon
found out.

It took a little time to iron out the wrinkles and make sure the
cane we were getting from Sharpe and Pezon Michelle was of the
right density and had been properly heat treated. We re-milled
the strips to final dimensions back in Vermont, on a machine that
milled to plus or minus one-half a thousandth of an inch.

We were quite certain that we were legally importing *manufactured* bamboo parts. The law read that a product principally
manufactured in a free country could be imported regardless of the

source of the original material. We were paying our two European
suppliers about twelve dollars for bamboo segments that they had
manufactured from a dollar's worth of raw bamboo, so clearly there
was considerable added value and the logical assumption was that
it was done by some kind of manufacturing process. But I had a
lot to learn about government and the law.

My education in these matters began when five men showed
up at my office; three from Foreign Assets Control and two from
the FBI. They had a subpoena that ordered my manager Clayton
Shappy and me to appear in Washington. I was to answer to the
charge of importing illegal material from China. I called John
Drinko, who hired a Washington lawyer, and we went down there
to see what it was all about.

There was a hearing before the assistant director of Foreign
Assets Control, which was part of the State Department. This
seemed like a lot of heavy artillery to use against one little fishing-
tackle company in Vermont that was making bamboo rods. Sort of
like a tank going after a country boy who is just doing a little
whittling. But it was pretty clear these men meant business. The
assistant director told us in very stern tones that he believed Orvis
had been knowingly and purposely breaking the law, and he was
going to prove it. The penalty was jail.

Our Washington lawyer was a man named Donald Hiss, who
was the brother of Alger Hiss of the notorious Hiss-Chambers case.
Donald Hiss did not back down from the assistant director. He went
right back at him, very aggressively, and he said something like,
"Don't you threaten my client. The last client you worked over
wound up floating in the Potomac River."

I inferred it was a suicide.

I probably looked a little apprehensive, because when we were
leaving, Hiss said, "Don't worry. I know how to handle this bird."

But I knew that even if he managed to keep me out of jail, I
was still going to be paying some pretty hefty legal fees. The irony
did not strike me then, but later I remembered that some of my
business friends in Cleveland thought I had made a mistake by

moving to Vermont. They saw me living at the end of a dirt road somewhere, pulling on my black and red wool jacket every day to go out and check the mail or do some work on my wood pile. I was leaving the mainstream, they thought, for the life of a quiet, small-time businessman. Well, the State Department evidently didn't think of Orvis as small time.

The case dragged on for several months, the way these things do, and got bogged down in little distinctions that really didn't amount to much, except that it cost a lot to argue about them. Foreign Assets Control claimed that our bamboo was merely "processed" in Europe, not "manufactured," and if they could prove it, we were in trouble. We learned that there were pages and pages of impenetrable bureaucratic prose that drew the distinction between manufactured and processed. I studied them, along with the lawyers, and we found that, according to one definition, a material that underwent a chemical change in the handling process was considered manufactured.

I asked for some help from David Ledlie, who was a trustee of the American Museum of Fly Fishing and a professor of chemistry at Middlebury College in Vermont and also a fine fly fisherman. David researched the subject for us and wrote a lengthy paper on the chemical changes that occur in bamboo during the heat-treating process. His conclusions supported our argument, and Orvis won the case. We were allowed to continue importing bamboo strips, but it had cost us some thirty thousand dollars in legal fees to get to that point. What it had cost the taxpayers is hard to determine but certainly several times that. The irony of the whole thing is that a week after the settlement, the United States' Ping-Pong team battered down the bamboo curtain, the embargo against China was lifted, and Orvis was free to import cane poles directly from China.

But that was not the end of my adventures in the bamboo trade. Even after the embargo was lifted, we weren't able to get bamboo. Deliveries were erratic, and quality was inconsistent.

Lou Marden, a writer with *National Geographic,* had access to China, and he was working on an article on bamboo. It was his idea for Orvis to make a rod for Chairman Mao. We sent it over and got something back saying that it had been received. I'm not sure he ever used it—fly-fishing probably wasn't a very proletarian sort of thing—but that wasn't the point. It opened a door for us so that we could get into China and deal directly with our suppliers.

Lou was very helpful in getting us visas to go to China. You had to be invited, so we asked for an invitation and we got one. We were very excited, and then, twenty-four hours later, we got a denial for the same request. But it didn't refer to the acceptance, so Lou said, "That's simple—throw away the denial and bring the acceptance."

So my wife and I went to China in 1975, and we stayed four days at the Spring Trade Fair in Kwangchow. I was told that this was the first time that a rod builder and a cane grower had ever met face to face to discuss their mutual interests. We thought we'd explain to the Chinese what we used the bamboo for. They had a huge goldfish pond near where we were meeting, so I rigged a rod and started casting. Well, immediately these Chinese guys came up and grabbed me and said, through the interpreter, "No, no. Those are the chairman's fish." It seems the chairman owned everything over there, and it didn't matter one bit that I didn't even have a hook on the end of that line so there was no way I was going to catch one of the chairman's fish. They weren't taking any chances.

That trip, then, was one of the few times I've ever traveled somewhere and not gotten in some fishing.

We made our needs known, and things actually did get better after that trip. But we never got to the point where deliveries of cane were reliable and consistent enough that we just stopped worrying about them until rod building had moved on to new space-age materials. Then we weren't utterly dependent, as rod builders, on *Arundinaria amabilis* anymore.

Chapter 6

The Catalog Is in the Mail

When I showed up in 1965, more than half of the business Orvis did was coming through dealers who sold our rods. We also had a few other products we were wholesaling, including a spinning reel, but those amounted to a small fraction of what the rods brought in. Another 12 percent came through our own store in Manchester. The rest, about 30 percent, came from catalog sales.

We did two mailings every year, sending out about fifty thousand catalogs in the spring and twenty thousand for the holiday season. I had a strong feeling that if we were going to grow, the catalog was the way to do it. I wanted to make the catalog more appealing, and I wanted to mail out more of them. A lot more.

When I arrived, the catalog was forty-eight pages, some of which were color, but most of it was still black and white. The catalog was laid out picture/copy, picture/copy, and it was pretty dull. I'm not a visual person, so I didn't have a lot of ideas about how to improve the look of the catalog. I knew it would take somebody else to breathe life into the pages. I just knew I wanted to provide more quality products for our customers and make more of them under the Orvis label, because we still had a lot of stuff under other companies' brand names. I wanted to develop proprietary products, specifically a complete line of fishing gear that would include everything from reel, lines, and leaders, to waders and clothes, and I wanted to expand the gift and lifestyle lines.

At the time, I didn't have the staff to do all that. There were only twenty people working there, and fourteen of them were down in the rod shop. We were so shorthanded that when it came time to send out the catalogs, we'd shut down the rod shop and put the rod makers to work stuffing and addressing envelopes.

Initially, I found most of the new products. But my greatest stroke of good luck during that time was meeting Baird Hall casually at a dinner party.

I didn't have a home of my own in Vermont at the time, which was about six months into my ownership of Orvis. My wife and family were still living in Cleveland, and I was renting a guest house that belonged to a woman named Edith Snare, a really wonderful, lively person who came from good old New England stock. She was a cousin of John Foster Dulles, and she lived in the neighboring town of Dorset, where she was quite an entertainer. People called her the Duchess of Dorset. She was having a dinner party one night and had invited me, but at the time the party was scheduled to begin, she was nowhere to be seen. Some of her guests were standing at her front door, so I thought the least I could do was let them in and get them something to drink while we were waiting for our hostess to arrive.

We went into the house, and after about twenty or thirty minutes, Edith walked in with her house guest, who was Baird Hall. She wasn't fazed at all about being late to her own dinner party. She went upstairs and changed out of her blue jeans and into a dress and put on a delightful dinner party.

I started talking to Baird that night and found out he ran a little Orvis dealership out of his kitchen closet in Hyde Park, Vermont. His interest was in ultra, ultra light spinning—two-pound test lines and that sort of thing—and I don't think he'd done much fly-fishing. He was very arthritic and didn't have much mobility, though he never let on that it slowed him down at all. He got to be a pretty good fly fisherman later on.

At the time, Baird was in a second-career phase of his life. He was about sixty, I'd guess, and had worked for some of the biggest advertising agencies in New York, and he was also a writer. He'd written a number of novels—he called them "light love for the slicks," and he could grind them out. He and his wife had lived on a boat for a while somewhere on the coast. He knew how to enjoy the good life, and he'd retired to Vermont and was doing some advertising consulting as well as running his little shop.

I virtually hired him that night, on the spot—or decided I wanted to, anyway. I liked him right away and was impressed by the things he said and the way he had of saying them. He knew how to choose his words to make an impression, and I knew that would be an asset.

Baird went to work for Orvis as a consultant, and immediately he began reworking the copy in the catalog so that it did more than just describe the product in nuts-and-bolts fashion. For example, he would describe what a rod could do and why it was just the thing for certain kinds of streams or conditions and make you feel like you just had to have it before you went fishing again. Then he brought in his wife, Steve, to do the art direction so that the catalog had some visual style and wasn't just picture/copy, picture/copy anymore. The two of them made an enormous difference in the way the catalog looked and read—and sold.

It wasn't easy (it never is), but some of the problems Baird had to deal with in those early days seem almost quaint now. We used one local photographer—the only one in town—and he had a problem with liquor. So on the morning of a shoot, Baird would have to go to this fellow's place and wake him up and get him into condition where he could hold his camera steady to make a shot. We didn't have the ready services of professional models, so we used local people—a lot of them employees—and some of them eventually became as recognizable to millions of people as some of the faces they saw on television.

One local woman, a very attractive blonde, posed in a cashmere robe, and that picture broke a lot of hearts. One writer even wrote a story, later, for a national magazine, lamenting her disappearance from the Orvis catalog.

I got a letter myself from a customer who was smitten with this woman. He wanted to get to know her better and wondered if I would give him her address. I wrote a letter not only giving my customer the woman's address but also telling him that she had just been divorced and would certainly appreciate hearing from interesting people like him. I told him that she liked to ride horses and some other personal details that I knew since the woman was a friend. I copied the letter to her, but I never sent the original. A couple of days later, she came storming into my office and told me, in very strong terms, that she could take care of her own love life, thank you very much.

I'm not sure she ever appreciated that little joke as much as I did.

Baird had strong opinions on what should and should not be in the catalog. He had very firm ideas about quality, and pretty soon he had become the conscience of the company. He wouldn't allow junk or gimmicks in "his" catalog. He had a phrase for the way people looked at the catalog. They handled it with "loving hands at home," and they didn't want cheap, useless clutter. I really saw this side of Baird after we started using an advertising agent from Atlantic City. He was a one-man operation and a real ramrod sort of fellow, whose specialty was in direct advertising for names to add to our list. This guy had a real cynical attitude that one part of me liked. He sold himself to me by saying that if your product is diapers, you don't talk about how good the diaper is for a baby's ass; you talk about how convenient it is for the mother. Because babies don't buy diapers. Baird just hated this guy's guts. But they were actually a great combination. There was a kind of creative tension there. Baird easily outlasted that guy. But the fireworks were interesting, and maybe even productive.

Every now and then, I would overrule Baird on something. I remember I found a Lucite toilet seat with salmon flies embedded in it, and I insisted that we put it in the catalog. Baird had a fit about that. It was definitely not his idea of the Orvis image. It turned out that we didn't sell many, either.

Not long after Baird started, I came up with the idea for the *Orvis News*. I asked him to be the editor. His first reaction was that house organs are duller than dishwater and are good only for the ego of the CEO.

"No, this isn't a house organ," I said. "This is a selling tool to the customer."

My idea was simple enough. Duckie had started something he called the Record Catch Club, which encouraged customers to send in pictures of themselves with fish they had caught on Orvis rods. What I wanted to do was put the Record Catch Club in a little newsprint publication, along with articles telling people where to fish, and how to fish, and what sort of tackle to use. We'd send the *News* out to people on our mailing list in between catalogs. It would keep them thinking about the company and make them feel like they were a part of something.

After I'd explained the idea, Baird took it on and made the *News* a tremendous success. He stayed with Orvis until his health wouldn't let him work anymore. But he never let his condition stop him as long as he was there. I remember that the back of his car was always smashed to hell. Even if it was a brand-new car, it was smashed to hell in a matter of days because he couldn't turn his head easily—he could barely turn it enough to see the side mirrors when he was driving. So his theory, when he was backing up, was to just keep on backing until he hit something. Then he'd go forward. Sometimes he hit harder than others. For obvious reasons no one wanted to drive with Baird.

But I remember one time when the kids were real young and we were going to take a canoe trip on the Lamoille River up where he lived. They said, "Say, Mr. Hall, why don't you come along with us?" It never occurred to them that he had any kind of disability that would keep him from doing just exactly what they were doing. He was that way. He had a young attitude.

I don't think anyone would argue against my strong belief that the success of any organization depends on the sum of the talent of the employees. Baird Hall was as instrumental to the success of Orvis as anyone who ever joined us. His footprints were all over everything we did in those early years. Especially the *News* and the catalog.

Making the catalog better and more inviting was only half the battle. We also needed to get it out to more people. We needed to add names to our mailing list. There were traditional ways of doing this—chiefly by advertising—but they were slow and expensive. We ran ads in various magazines, including *The New Yorker,* and we would get some responses. We'd mail out a few more catalogs and add a few more names to the list. We did one promotion in which you could buy some flies by filling out one of those perforated cards you find sticking in magazines and mailing it in. This was the Orvis nymph selection—nymphs being a kind of underwater fly—and it was a success. We got some names that way. But it was slow going. I wanted to move a lot faster, and I had an idea for how to do it.

I came up with a plan to exchange lists with our competitors. Orvis would send catalogs to a large sample from L.L. Bean's list and vice versa; then we would measure the results. There would be some overlap, and some of their people wouldn't be interested in our catalog. But the odds were that a lot of people would be. Catalog shopping was in its infancy, and there were plenty of people who would look at an unfamiliar catalog and, if it struck their fancy, order something. To my knowledge, there was no such thing as list brokers at the time, so I decided to call on the people who were my competitors—Bean, Norm Thompson, Abercrombie & Fitch, Eddie Bauer, and an outfit called Alaska Sleeping Bag—and make my pitch.

Well, the only place where I received even polite interest was Abercrombie & Fitch, and we had a relationship with them already.

They were selling our rods in their retail stores and even put them in their catalog from time to time. So Abercrombie gave me a hearing. But everybody else threw me out on my ear. In fact, I literally got thrown out of Eddie Bauer. I had made an appointment with the man who was in charge of marketing. His name was Bill McGuire, and I was sitting in his office, where we were getting along famously, when Eddie Bauer himself walked by. He called McGuire over and said, "Who is that guy?"

McGuire explained that I was from Orvis, and we were discussing trading lists.

"Well, throw him the hell out," Bauer said, loud enough so I could hear it.

McGuire was a nice guy and terribly embarrassed. But he did have to ask me to leave.

But I was an old salesman, and rejection was something I knew how to live with. I kept making the rounds, talking about trading lists. Within three years, we were all trading or renting each other's lists, to everyone's benefit. Of course, the practice is standard in mail order these days, which is why you get catalogs from companies you've never heard from before. You ordered one catalog, and this strange new company got your name when it rented your name from the catalog you bought from.

There is one more interesting footnote to this story. After a couple of years, Abercrombie decided to stop trading lists with us. Their explanation was that we were doing better than they were. The reason was that they were locked into a retail mentality and put products in their catalog only when they wouldn't move in their stores.

Abercrombie & Fitch had been a great company with strong name identification going back to when they were outfitters for celebrities going on African safaris. They had this image that made you think of Teddy Roosevelt and Ernest Hemingway, and they were in a far better position to advance the upscale sporting market than Orvis in the days when I had just taken over the company. But they didn't know how to handle the new world of mail order. They were also mismanaged and went through five different presidents in my first seven years at Orvis.

When I acquired Orvis, Abercrombie was by far our largest customer. They bought between 10 and 15 percent of our rods. But things went downhill for them, and, even though they had customer acceptance, they were losing money. I remember being called into a meeting with their last president, who was also a major owner. He was the whole package, right down to the English secretary with the old-school accent who kept me waiting twenty minutes past my appointment to see him. I was barely in my chair before he said, "What's the matter with Orvis?"

He had a sheet of paper in front of him with figures on it showing that we had supplied them with a lot more rods in the previous year than we had in the current year. He went on to imply, not very subtly, that I was doing a lousy job of running Orvis and that I had better shape up.

Well, I had always said that the customer was always right, even when you knew damn well he was wrong, and that when you got a complaint, what you did was say, "You're right, we're wrong, and we're going to fix it."

But this time I made an exception. Maybe I had been in Vermont too long and a little of that Yankee attitude had worn off on me.

"Let me tell you what's wrong with Orvis," I told the CEO. "Seven years ago, when Abercrombie & Fitch was being supplied a large number of rods, you were 15 percent of our business. In the meantime, we've grown tenfold, and we don't ship to you because you don't pay your bills. *That* is what's the matter with Orvis."

I don't think he ever figured out what the matter with Orvis was. And he didn't figure out what the matter with Abercrombie's was, either. Not long after that, they closed their doors.

Getting rod production up was one challenge when I started running Orvis. Making the catalog more attractive and getting more of them in the mail was another. Changing some attitudes was also a challenge and, in some ways, the most interesting one I faced.

My predecessor at Orvis, Duckie Corkran, would start his day by going to the post office, just across the street from the office, and picking up the mail. Then he would come back to the office and open the mail—each and every letter, by hand, himself. And if there was a complaint, he would shout down the hall to somebody he thought was responsible or could fix the problem. They had one of those pneumatic devices to move interoffice mail from one floor to another, and that included customer orders. Every now and then one of the canisters that held the order would get stuck in the tube. It was very old-fashioned, to say the least, even for Vermont.

This was before the credit card became the all-purpose shopping tool that it is today. Orvis didn't have banks of phone operators sitting at computer terminals, taking orders. We had a few people who came into the store and paid cash. Some people—very good customers—had charge accounts and might call in an order and say "charge it." But there weren't many of those. And then there were the people who got the catalog in the mail and sent in their order with a check. One day, I found a cardboard box full of uncashed checks. I asked the bookkeeper what the story was on those checks.

"Those are from people who've ordered something that we haven't been able to ship yet."

You mean, I asked her, that you wait until you actually mail the item before you deposit the check?

"Well, yes," she said, "of course." Her tone made it pretty plain that she believed to do otherwise would be dishonest. I told her to take those checks on down to the bank and deposit them. I consoled her by adding that we would scrupulously refund the customers' money if we couldn't ship their orders in a reasonable time.

It was that kind of place.

I wanted to change that. I *had* to change it if I was going to get anywhere with my plans. To do this, I needed to get good people in the right positions. I looked around the office and spotted one fellow who seemed to have all his work done about thirty minutes after the office opened and then put his feet up on the desk and waited for something to come along. I figured he must have some ability and plenty of confidence so I started giving him more responsibility, and pretty soon he was treasurer of the company and then general manager. Clayton Shappy stayed with Orvis until his untimely death in May 1991.

When Clayton moved up to general manager, we hired a young man from the Bronx, Tom Vaccaro, to be treasurer. Tom didn't know anything about fishing, hunting, or country living, but he wanted to learn. He found out about us through the *Orvis News*. We hired him in 1978, and he has grown in his job tremendously and helped the company grow. He is now CFO, and he knows far more about fly-fishing and country living now than he did when he started. But he sounds like he never left the Bronx, and that still tickles some of the old Vermonters in the office, who, for some reason, don't think there is anything funny at all about *their* accent.

Incidentally, I got another lesson in the wisdom of going with your gut feeling on matters of personnel when Tom Vaccaro brought Joe Cassidy in as his replacement in the position of controller. Joe is a big, red-headed Irishman, very quiet and very bright. He did a first-rate job as controller, but by 1988 he was burned out and prepared to leave if we didn't have another job for him. Neither Tom nor I wanted to lose Joe, so I suggested making him VP of marketing.

Joe was the last person most people would have picked for a marketing role. He has zero capacity for bullshit and a slightly skeptical—if not downright negative—attitude. On the other hand, mail order is a highly statistical business, and Joe is a wizard as a statistics analyst.

Well, it turned out that Tom and I couldn't have made a better decision. Some of our greatest late-growth years were due to

Joe's ability to analyze and segment our mailing list and to target these segments with offerings that dovetailed with their purchasing histories. Orvis—like Joe—is smiling a lot more since he became VP of marketing.

A business is like a chain. There is always a weak link, and once that is fixed, the next weakest link shows up. For a long time, order fulfillment was our weak link at Orvis, in large part because we were growing so fast. That all turned around when Tom Vaccaro found John Moticha, who became VP of operations and, through great people skills and an incredible sense of organization, made fulfillment one of our strongest links. So Tom was not just a good find but also a good finder.

In the early years, we got a lot of people like Tom Vaccaro, who were attracted to Orvis by the *News*. We advertised, occasionally, in the *News* for people to fill positions, and we always got a lot of applications. The *News* and the catalog were starting to get out to more and more people as the list kept growing and growing. And the *News* and the catalog were creating and selling the image of a life that a lot of people found very attractive. It wasn't the fishing and hunting alone, though that was certainly the foundation for all of it.

What we were creating and selling was, for lack of a better word, a lifestyle. It is an appreciation of the outdoors and country living, a kind of Americanized version of elegant, English country living, and things like tweeds and dogs were all a part of it. A feeling for that kind of life came across in both the catalog and the *News,* and it hit a nerve. We had found not just a niche but an identity. We could feel it, and as the company began to grow and new people came in, I think a lot of the people working for Orvis could sense it too. It was an exciting place to work. I know *I* certainly found it exciting.

I was always looking for ways to capitalize on this sense of identity, this feeling that many of our customers had of being more than just consumers but of actually being part of something. That's what the Record Catch Club in the *News* was about. People who used Orvis equipment and had caught a fish they were proud of would send in a picture, and we'd publish it in the *News* so other customers who used Orvis tackle could admire it. It wasn't like bragging to strangers, which is gauche. This was bragging to your club, which is perfectly acceptable. With half a million copies of the *News* going out, it wasn't exactly an exclusive club. But because there was a *News* and it did publish the pictures people sent in, there was the feeling of being more than just an anonymous, replaceable consumer and customer. We were delighted and proud that people felt that way, and I wanted to build on it.

One of the best ideas I had for doing this came to me when I was on one of my trips to Europe, when I was looking for a reliable source of bamboo. I noticed that in England there were a number of schools where you could go for a couple of days to learn how to use a fly rod. Nobody, after all, is born knowing how. If you don't have a father—or, as in my case, a mother—to teach you when you are young, then you either teach yourself and develop all sorts of bad habits that are hard to break or find a friend who may, or may not, know what he is talking about. Very few friends, even if they can teach the skill, have the patience to do it, and it is next to impossible to teach a spouse to fly-fish. Most Americans wouldn't consider taking up skiing, tennis, or golf, for instance, without going through a couple of days of beginner's classes and maybe then some private lessons from an instructor. But in the time when I'd just taken over Orvis, when it came to fly-fishing, you were on your own. It seemed to me that if we were going to be selling that equipment—and the joys of that sport—to our customers, we ought to be teaching them how to use it and get the most out of it, too.

So one day I went to see Dick Finlay, the man I'd called about buying Orvis, and told him that I wanted him, and another man named Bill Cairns, to start a fishing school. Dick was a good ski instructor—he'd trained the troops of the 10th Mountain Division during World War II—and Bill was the finest fly fisherman I knew. I was certain that the two of them could come up with a good program for teaching fly-fishing to novices, even though they were, in typical Vermont fashion, skeptical about the whole idea.

"Well," I said, "let's give it a try. We'll advertise it in the *News* and see if we can't get a dozen people."

I told them to plan for that many, anyway, and we'd just hope we got them.

Well, within ten days of mailing the *News,* we had over 150 applicants. And most of them had called in. This was in 1967, when people didn't use the phone to call in orders. But they were so excited about the schools that they wanted to make sure they got in on them.

Bill Cairns became the head of the program and geared up for a full summer of schools, which were very popular. He made a lot of friends, who remember him, with affection, as the person who taught them how to fly cast. I never planned for the schools to be big moneymakers—I always saw them as more sizzle than steak—but they did help us with our retail sales that year. When the people came up to Manchester to go through the three-day school, they would inevitably go into the store and find something they needed. Some people who had never fished—or never fly-fished, anyway—would come to the school, and after they had learned on school equipment and decided that this was something they liked doing, they would go in the store and completely outfit themselves. This, of course, had been part of my plan.

That first year, we ran several schools in Manchester, using mostly employees from the company for instructors, as well as some local people who were friends of the company and good fishermen. We graduated about 150 people. So the schools were a success, and they began to grow like the rest of the company. We added people, and when we did, we found that it was often easier to hire someone who already knew how to teach—a ski instructor from one of the nearby mountains, for example—and then teach him how to fish, than it was to take a fisherman who didn't have the personality for teaching and make an instructor out of him. We were interested in instructors who could deal with people, in other words. We wanted this to be a good experience for our customers, one that would leave them with positive feelings about the company.

In addition to adding staff, we also conducted the schools in more locations. At first, it was just Manchester. Soon, we began a school down in Pennsylvania, around Harrisburg and the Yellow Breeches River, because that is where one of our key employees, a man named Tony Skilton came from. Tony had worked his way through college by tying flies and selling them wholesale to Orvis. He came to work for us after graduation and became one of our most valuable employees. He died of cancer, tragically, when he was still a very young man. He was an outstanding angler and a very good instructor who is remembered by a lot of people who went through the schools.

After that first experiment with conducting schools away from Manchester, we went all out. Now we have them in Evergreen, Colorado; Coeur d'Alene, Idaho; Cape Cod; and Key Largo, as well as in Manchester, where we have schools running from spring right through the summer. We have schools that are for women only. And, of course, we have plenty of imitators. Last year, about twenty-four hundred people went through our fishing schools.

The fishing schools have been, easily, one of our most successful innovations. In fact, they were so successful that I copied them myself and started a shooting school in 1973. The idea was the same, and, in some ways, the need was greater. If you don't already know how to shoot a shotgun, then you certainly need to be properly taught. For safety, if for no other reason.

And if you are an American sportsman and you already know how to shoot a shotgun, you probably don't do it properly and you could improve your shooting considerably with the right kind of instruction. Most Americans who grew up learning to shoot did so on a rifle. So they know how to aim. But in wing shooting, you don't aim. You concentrate on the target, and, if you have mounted your gun properly and it fits—which is very important—you will hit what you are looking at.

This is the way the British have approached shotgunning for years and years. It is called instinctive shooting, and it works. But a lot of American shooters take some convincing. Especially on the business about the fit of the gun.

Thanks to the opportunities I'd had to shoot in Scotland, I realized how much better the average British shotgunner was than his American counterpart. There was a good reason for this. They took their shooting very seriously, and almost all of them went to one of the several shooting schools in England, on a regular basis, to improve and polish their skills. When I decided to start Orvis schools in the United States, my first move was to go over there and enroll in the West London shooting school to see what it was all about. I was very impressed, and my own shooting certainly improved. And based on what I'd seen, I thought we could do an even better job at Orvis.

The British schools are designed primarily to prepare you for the classic driven shoots, where the birds are being pushed toward you and you take mostly incoming shots. In my experience, most quality upland shooting in the United States is for flushing birds over pointing dogs, and, though incoming shots are important, outgoing and covey explosions are crucial. We would need to make that a consideration in the Orvis method.

I had considered finding a British instructor to come over and run our school, but, with the difference in styles in mind, the more I thought about it, the less I liked the idea. Besides, I was having trouble finding a candidate. When I announced to my staff that I was going to start a shooting school and was looking for someone to head it up, Ben Upson, who was managing our retail store, came to see me. He told me, in all modesty, that he was sure he could handle the job. I had a great deal of respect for Ben, and I knew he'd been a good instructor at our fly-fishing schools, but I didn't realize what a talented shot he was.

I found out, fairly quickly, and was reminded of something no businessman should forget—namely, that there is often a lot of talent in your organization that is waiting to be discovered and that you don't necessarily have to go looking outside for people when you decide to take on something new. When you go inside, you have the advantage of dealing with someone who already knows your company and the way it does things and whose loyalty will grow with increased responsibility. Ben's certainly did. He ran the shooting school for many years before he retired. He was a great instructor who believed he could teach anyone to shoot. I saw him teach a man with one arm to shoot very competently. Ben did it by shooting one armed himself and showing the fellow that it could be done. He was also very good at teaching women to shoot, of getting them over their fear of guns and their embarrassment at missing.

When he came to work for us, Ben was on his second career, having retired as an undertaker. He was a burly guy with a big laugh and a good sense of humor. Once a bunch of us were down at my place in Florida for some quail shooting. It was midwinter, December or January, the best time of year for Gulf Coast oysters. We had picked up some from Apalachicola and were opening them and eating them at night before we sat down to dinner, and my old friend and director Dick Whitney ate a bad oyster. He was in agony all night and didn't make it up for reveille.

In the morning, we were all going out early for some duck hunting. Ben looked in on Dick, and when he came out of the room, he was really concerned.

"You know," he said, "Dick looks really bad. In fact, I believe I've buried people who looked better than he does."

I'm glad to report that we did not have to bury Dick. He recovered and lived on, just like that quip of Ben's.

I sent Ben and another employee named Bruce Bowlen to enroll in three British schools: West London, Holland & Holland, and

John Mayo. They came back full of enthusiasm, certain that they could run an even better school for the American market. They recruited some other instructors from the staff, built a school on property near my house on the Battenkill River, and opened for business in 1973.

The first step in working with the students was to fit them for proper gun measurements. We did this with a tri-gun that had an adjustable stock for length of pull, drop and comb, pitch, and cast on or off (the way the stock is bent, slightly, left or right). When it is mounted correctly (a vital teaching point), a properly fit gun will point exactly where the gunner is looking. Most of our students were amazed when we'd have them shoulder a tri-gun and immediately shoot at a target—not taking time to aim. If they were missing, they invariably missed in the same place—lower left, say, or lower right—every time. By adjusting the dimensions of the tri-gun, we'd have them hitting the bull's-eye every time. It makes a very persuasive case for the fitted shotgun and, not so incidentally, a great case for Orvis gunsmithing to refit an existing gun or, even better, an Orvis custom-made Spanish or Italian gun.

Like the fishing schools, the Orvis shooting schools were a great success. We could take a maximum of sixteen students, and even with that small number, safety was a serious concern. But Ben Upson came up with the perfect solution. The instructors carried the shells and actually loaded them into the gun. That way, they always knew whether a gun was loaded or not. Today, twenty-six years later, we have never had an accident, with five thousand students having gone through our schools.

That's not to say we haven't had problems. One of the givens in business is that you will have problems. The test is how you deal with them.

Our first hurdle with the shooting schools was in acquiring a permit. This involved a town meeting, with all sorts of people attending to offer their opinions. At first, I didn't think things were going very well for our side. Some of the Green Mountain boys from the local "hook and bullet" club showed up and said they didn't see a lot of reasons that Orvis should be teaching fancy folks from New York how to come up and shoot "their" birds. There was a lot of nodding and murmuring of agreement with that sentiment. Then, some little newcomer to the state, a man who had relocated to Bennington from somewhere in New Jersey, stood up and said that he thought it was perfectly terrible for Orvis to be teaching people to kill poor little animals. As soon as I heard that, I knew we had the ballgame won. It was in the bag. The Green Mountain boys immediately came over to our side. They weren't going to have some flatlander wimp telling them they shouldn't be hunting. For that matter, they began to believe that Orvis ought to be teaching *more* people how to hunt.

The next problem came when a neighbor, and not a very close neighbor at that, complained that the noise from all the shooting was bothering him. Even though he was half a mile away and other people were closer, we decided to be a good neighbor and move the school. I went to see him and told him about our plan—which, by the way, involved costs of about seventy thousand dollars—and that the new location would be about twice as far from his home as the previous one had been and that there would now be a low ridge between his home and the school.

About a year later, he complained again.

This time, our choice was between closing down the Manchester school or taking him on in court, which we did.

We hired one lawyer from Rutland, Vermont, and another from Columbus, Ohio, and also an acoustics expert from the University of Vermont, who took sound testings and testified that the noise at our opponent's house was no more than that of a bicycle— not a motor bike—passing by.

He hired a very tough lawyer, and his expert witness was a health guru who testified that the noise of the shooting school was, to our opponent, like Chinese water torture, the constant drip, drip, drip causing him emotional distress, which included impotence.

We ran the school only during the day. In fact, we kept normal working hours, eight to five. It turned out that our adversary was a retired big-city policeman who had come to the country and hung out his shingle as a private investigator. I don't know how much of a market there was for his kind of services in a little country town of less than four thousand people. Maybe he had too much time on his hands.

Anyway, we finally settled on the courthouse steps, with a cash payment and an agreement not to shoot on Sundays or after 5 P.M. on weekdays. We also put in a lot of expensive acoustical sound barriers to muffle the noise.

We never learned—and didn't want to—how this worked out for our antagonist. But the arrangement certainly caused some inconvenience to us and to some of our potential customers. Before the court settlement, we could take people up to the school area for private shooting lessons. But we had to stop doing that, which meant that we had to say no to people who wanted one-on-one instruction. One of those happened to be Dan Rather, the newscaster. We had planned on giving him personal instruction, but then we made that deal with our neighbor and had to cancel.

Still, the shooting school has been a great success, and we now conduct them at other locations, including Florida and Millbrook, New York. One of the marked differences between the fishing and shooting schools is that very few people ever return to the fishing school once they have learned the basics of casting and knot tying. They can pretty much go on their own after that for self-improvement. In the shooting school, on the other hand, we have many repeat customers who want to get tuned up, almost on an annual basis, for the shooting season. Both schools are excellent sizzle for Orvis, and we make a lot of first-name friends and add a great deal to our image of quality and credibility in the fields.

Some people are surprised to learn that about 25 percent of our shooting students are women. One lady came to our shooting schools nine years in a row until she finally got what she was looking for—a sporting gentleman to marry. The Orvis shooting school got the job done.

* * *

Those early years, when I was just getting up to speed, were busy times but also exciting times. There's nothing quite like the feeling that comes with building something. You try things and you don't know if they're going to work out, and when they do, there is just this feeling of pride and accomplishment. Of course, it is also important to put a stop loss on your good ideas that don't work. You have to let the evidence overrule your pride. In the mail-order business you get a very quick reading on ideas and products that don't work. That is just one more example of how the customer is always right.

Everybody says that the great days in the history of any business come during the entrepreneurial phase of things, and that was certainly my experience. You are just full of ideas, and even when you are away from the business and supposedly doing something else, you are thinking about ways to make the business better and more competitive. You find ways to make it grow or new quality products to offer to your customers and ways to make old products better.

I'll give you an example. One of my best ideas for a new Orvis product came to me one day at lunch, while I was staring at a waitress's chest.

This is going to take some explaining.

When I started at Orvis, there was only one place in Manchester to eat lunch, and that was the Coburn House, a pleasant, homey, old New England hotel right in the middle of town. Duckie Corkran would often join us there for lunch, during which he would carry on a feud with a crusty old waitress by the name of Lil. They were always at each other, never a pleasant word, and it wasn't really good natured. They meant it. One day when I was sitting next to Duckie, Lil spilled a whole bowl of pea soup in my lap, and her only expression of regret was to say, "Sorry, young fella. I meant to dump that on Corkran."

Well, one day, we were at lunch and being served by a refreshing alternative to Lil, an attractive young woman named Mavis, who got quite flustered when I kept staring at her chest. What got my attention was this little retrievable reel with a pencil on it for taking orders. When she needed the pencil, she could pull the string out all the way and write down her order. When she was finished, the string was pulled back into this little cartridge by a spring-loaded device. The string was out of the way, but the pencil was handy when she needed it again.

I kept staring at that gizmo and thinking it was a product that would appeal to every fly fisherman in the world.

When you are standing in a trout stream, in water up to your waist, and you need to trim your leader, you use a small set of nippers that look like ordinary nail clippers. If you are nervous because there are fish rising and you want to hurry up and change flies and get back to fishing, or if your fingers are a little cramped from lots of casting or cold from the water, then you might very well fumble those nippers and drop them in the water. If you tie them to your vest with a length of line, then that line will inevitably blow around and get in the way when you least need for that to happen. With a retractable device like the waitress was using to keep track of her pencil, the tool would always be there when you needed it. You couldn't drop it in the water, and the keeper string would be out of the way when you weren't using it.

Fly fishermen tumbled to the tool right away once we started offering it. It made such obvious sense. We put the name Orvis on the little stainless-steel cylinder that held the retracted line, so whenever you saw a fly fisherman, you saw the name of the company, pinned to his chest. This was in 1967, long before people began putting company names or logos on every piece of equipment or clothing they sold. So we got our name on every fly fisherman's chest, and we also added to a reputation for innovation and for understanding the needs of our customers, right down to the small things, which can seem like the most important things of all when you've just dropped your only pair of nippers, or your flashlight, into the river.

This was probably my first innovative contribution to the world of fly-fishing. We called it the Zinger, and we've sold millions of them. Today, Orvis sells Zingers in five different styles, including one that contains a retractable tape measure so you can measure your fish before you release it.

One last note to that story: Mavis went to work for Orvis and became a valuable and effective employee.

When you are starting, you don't miss much, and everything is grist for the mill.

Chapter 7

Worldwide Sportsman

While the first few years were very busy, I wasn't exactly chained to my desk. I had a feeling, even back then, that the world of sport, for Orvis customers, was expanding way beyond the local stream where they had always fished. I was eager to see some of this expanding world and to check out the fishing. When I came back, I could report on it, in the *Orvis News,* so our customers could go themselves. Like they say, it was a tough job, but somebody had to do it.

One of the first of many memorable sporting trips that I took in my years at Orvis came about a year after I took over the company. I went to Argentina as a guest of the legendary angler Joe Brooks and his wife, Mary.

When I acquired Orvis, the two giants of the fly-fishing world were Joe Brooks and Lee Wulff. They were both expert anglers who traveled the world, catching trophy fish and writing about it for the sporting magazines. They were both striking-looking men, and everyone who fly fished knew what they looked like and admired them the way kids worship their favorite baseball players. As it turned out, both of them had some connection with Orvis.

At one time, Lee Wulff lived in New York State, right across the line and just downstream on the Battenkill from Manchester and Orvis. So he was almost a neighbor. He had fished with Orvis rods for most of his life. Early in my Orvis days, I made a lunch date with him to see if we could formalize a relationship and possibly have a rod, or even a series of rods, named after him. In fishing, as in everything else, the endorsement of people who have authority in the field counts for a lot.

Now, I was a great admirer of Lee, but it became quickly apparent at that lunch that it was not mutual. At least not where Orvis was concerned. He complained to me that Duckie Corkran had told him that he would be made a director of Orvis and never followed through. As a result, he wasn't interested in having anything further to do with the Orvis company. Like many very talented people, he was proud and sort of remote. As an angler, he is remembered for many accomplishments—like the Wulff tied dry flies—and for his tireless articulation of the catch-and-release philosophy. Wulff was famous for saying, "A trout is too valuable to be caught only once." But he was a man to admire and not necessarily one to be friendly with.

Joe Brooks was the other thing completely. He was a giant of a man, in many ways. He was physically large and totally generous. He was a thoughtful man, whose attitude about fly-fishing was anything but elitist—which there was a lot of in those days. Joe believed that fly-fishing was for everyone, and that it wasn't difficult to learn. He was every man and woman's fly-fishing hero.

I was thrilled to be fishing with him in Argentina, where it was quickly apparent to me that his reputation was possibly even greater than it was back in the States. He had pioneered fly-fishing in Argentina, which has some of the best trout fishing and most beautiful rivers in the world, and was just about single-handedly responsible for establishing the ethic of catch-and-release in that country.

I got an indelible lesson into that way of thinking, myself, on that trip. We were fishing the Chimehuin River, primarily, and also the Malleo, my all-time favorite river. The big thing was to fish the Boca of the Chimehuin, where the large brown and rainbow trout collected before spawning. World-record fish had been caught there by Joe Brooks and other celebrated anglers, like Billy Pate. But it was slow fishing.

One day I decided to go off by myself, downriver, to see if I could find a little more productive water. I had not been indoctrinated into catch-and-release and was still in the habit of killing an occasional fish. I was fortunate enough to catch a five-and-a-half-pound brown trout, which I promptly killed. A little later, I caught another of about seven pounds. I killed that one, also. These were the two largest trout I had ever caught, by quite a large margin. I was tickled to death and came strolling back to join the other anglers like the conquering hero. I could tell, however, from the looks I got that the others saw me a little differently. No one said I shouldn't have killed the fish. No one had to. I got the picture.

I've been a catch-and-release man from that day on.

I remember another incident from that trip. After a day of fishing the Chimehuin, we were taking our rods down, and I was having real trouble separating the ferrules of my bamboo rod. Joe Brooks, a big, powerful man, tried to help me. The two of us were pushing and pulling, in the proper cross-handed fashion, but we couldn't get the rod apart. Joe called to his wife, Mary, who was already in the car. She came over to lend a hand, but she was a small lady, and I couldn't imagine what she could accomplish.

Joe handed her the rod and said, "Would you please take this apart?"

She took the rod and, with little apparent effort, separated it and handed it back to Joe, who smiled and said, "Okay, dear. You can get back in the car now."

The rivers in Argentina resemble those in Montana and Wyoming, and the fishing was probably like it had been in the Rockies fifty years ago, before the boom in fly-fishing. I had done a fair amount of fly-fishing before I went down to Argentina, and I was no novice. But I had never experienced trout fishing like this before. Most days we had the river entirely to ourselves, except for the occasional Indian fishing for food with a length of monofilament line wrapped around a tin can. The ends of the tin can would be cut off

so the fisherman could stick his lower arm through it and then roll
the line up quickly or point his arm in the direction he wanted to
cast, fling the line in a circle above his head, and then let the line
pay off the can just like it was an open-faced spinning reel. They
could make amazingly long—and accurate—casts using this method,
and they caught some nice fish on frog legs.

We used flies, and I quickly discovered that these fish could
be just as fussy and selective as any. I was using flies that had
worked for me in the States. Some worked here, and some didn't.
You inevitably break off flies, some on fish and some on rocks or
other obstacles, and, since there was no place to pick up replace-
ments, I found myself worrying about running out of the flies that
did work. The fish were big, which is one reason for worrying about
losing flies. That seven-pounder and the five-and-a-half-pounder
that I caught, and unwisely killed, were taken within a half dozen
casts of each other. Now, there were a lot of very good anglers in
the States who had never caught a single trout over five pounds,
which tells you just how magnificent the fishing in Argentina is.

I caught those fish on a fly that was totally out of character for
the river. It was a big, gaudy saltwater fly I happened to be carrying, called a Honey Blonde. I was using it because Joe Brooks had
told me that when the fish weren't moving to the usual fly patterns,
you could sometimes stir them up and provoke a strike by using
something that startles them and offends their sensibilities. He
called it an "insult pattern," and he made a believer out of me.

After that trip—and another I took with him to Montana—
Joe wrote me with a proposal. He would represent the Orvis company for six thousand dollars a year. He already used our rods, so
he wasn't selling out. It would probably have been good for both of
us. Joe Brooks had such tremendous credibility in the fly-fishing
community that to have him connected formally with Orvis certainly couldn't have hurt, especially in the early days.

I thought it was a good idea. But I thought I'd better check
with Duckie Corkran, since he had more experience than I did in
dealing with outdoor writers, who had a reputation for coming

around with a hand out, looking for equipment and not offering much in return.

"Don't do it," Duckie said.

If you sign one, he felt, then you would become an enemy of all the others. So I decided to turn Joe down, and I've regretted it ever since. That six thousand dollars wasn't much to pay for the kind of good will he would have spread around for Orvis.

At the end of that first, wonderful week in Argentina, Joe had to go off somewhere to work on the television program *ABC's Wide World of Sports*. He recommended that the rest of us in his party stop on our way back to Buenos Aires at the Traful River, which was owned by the LaRiviera family. There were no telephones in the area, so it was impossible to call ahead, but Joe assured us that it would be no problem. So four of us drove up to this beautiful *estancia,* knocked on the door, announced ourselves, mentioned Joe's name, and said we'd like to do some fishing.

The senior LaRiviera promptly invited us in for lunch and insisted we spend the night. After lunch, I was taken to what I'm sure was the Traful's most productive pool, where I caught a ten-pound salmon on a size #10 Green Highlander. At the time, I thought the Traful had to be the most beautiful place I'd ever seen. The river is surrounded by mountains that resemble the Tetons in Wyoming, the water is a beautiful, turquoise blue, and in the sky you will occasionally see soaring condors, the largest flying birds in the world.

Thirty-three years later, I am still sure the Traful is the world's most beautiful place. My Florida neighbor Ted Turner evidently agrees with me, as he recently acquired it, and I'm glad, because I'm sure he will preserve it.

The trip to Argentina set a lot of standards in my mind for what good sporting travel should be like. The people were friendly and enthusiastic sportsmen. And the food—especially the local beef—

was as good as anyone could imagine. Sport, especially when you are traveling, isn't merely a question of catching fish or shooting game. There is also the matter of what people like to call the amenities.

I don't necessarily need luxury hotels and four-star restaurants when I am traveling. In fact, I like camping out and cooking over a fire. But when you go someplace like Argentina, where the amenities are supposed to be part of the experience, then you notice things, and you appreciate it when they are done right. And they do things right in Argentina. The people are wonderfully hospitable and take pride in service, which is not necessarily true, I've found, all over the world.

But the sport is the thing, and on that first trip with Joe Brooks, we had such great fishing I knew I wanted to return to Argentina. And I have, fourteen times, to be exact, and not just for the fishing. There is also excellent duck and bird hunting in Argentina. The dove shooting was a real eye-opener, the first time I tried it.

In the United States, dove shooting can be fast and furious, with the birds coming into a field to feed in great numbers on bennie or sunflowers or some other kind of grain. The birds are fast, but probably not as fast as a lot of frustrated shooters tend to think they are. Many ducks, for that matter, fly faster than doves. But a dove is nimble and quick and flies erratically and can be very hard to hit if you are just an average shooter. A busy dove field can be challenging and humbling to someone who thinks of himself as a pretty good shot. I had grown up shooting dove around the family place in Georgia, and I had seen days when so many birds came into a field that it was relatively easy to shoot a limit of twelve or fifteen birds.

But I had never seen anything like the dove shooting in Argentina, where the birds are so abundant that they are considered pests, especially around the grain-rich areas. There is no limit and no closed season, and you shoot until you are literally tired of shooting. In the United States, on a hot dove field, you might shoot two or three boxes of shells. In Argentina, you can easily shoot a case or two of shells. You can start picking your shots and try to make only those shots that you find especially difficult, like those that are straight overhead or hard crossing. Often as not, you simply shoot until you get tired of shooting or your arm is sore. After a couple of days of this kind of dove shooting, I've usually had enough; so I try to combine a dove-hunting trip with a fishing trip, which can be easily done.

An even better combination is to link the last week of trout season with the first week of duck season. This would usually be the second and third weeks of April, when Vermont is in the period called mud season and is a good place to get away from. Because it is in the Southern Hemisphere, Argentina's seasons are reversed, so that would be early fall down there, with the leaves changing and the air turning cooler. There duck hunting is wonderful, and you can shoot eleven different species, none of which we have in the United States.

One of the first times I went duck hunting in Argentina, I was shooting about a dozen ducks a day. They were coming in to decoys and to calls, and I couldn't have been happier, but one of the guides said we were a little early and that the best duck shooting would be coming up a little later in the season. Then, he added, we could count on getting a limit, which was twenty-five ducks a day.

In the United States, at that time, the limit was three.

So my first major sporting trip, after I took over Orvis, was an unqualified success. And I suppose that explains why I traveled so much after that and why I still go off all over the world today looking for some new place with great fishing or hunting. You never know, it may turn out to be as good as that first trip to Argentina, and, even if it isn't, it is always a great thrill to experience new waters and new country. I can't imagine ever getting tired of it.

A couple of years after that trip to Argentina, I went down to Cozumel, Mexico, with my kids, on what was essentially a family vacation. My wife, Mary, and I were recently divorced, and she had been scheduled to make the trip with the kids. When she fell ill, I took her place. We had a good time, snorkeling, scuba diving, and living the beach life, and sometime during the trip, I learned about a new fishing camp called Boca Paila. It was on the mainland, about a half hour flight from Cozumel.

You had to charter a plane, and you landed on a remote, dirt strip where there was nothing, not a single structure of any kind. Not even a lean-to for shade or cover if it rained. That's all changed now because so many people come to see the nearby Mayan ruins. Things are considerably more built up, with hourly buses running on roads that are paved all the way to Cancún and curio booths clustered around the ruins. But in 1968 it was desolate. We waited there for about twenty minutes after our plane took off and headed back for Cozumel, thinking we might be in a jungle survival situation.

Finally, Tony Gonzales, the proprietor of the resort, showed up in a jeep and took us to Boca Paila on a road that was so bad it took about an hour and a half to cover twenty-five miles. There were four of us—me; my eldest son, Ralph; his brother Leigh Jr., whom we called Perk; and sister Molly. We didn't know what to expect, and we were very pleasantly surprised.

The resort was clean and comfortable with nice cabins, built of palms like the Mayan homes, on a beautiful, ten-mile-long coral beach with clear water. Even the food was good. But in this case, it was not the amenities that made the trip special. What really got our attention was the flats fishing.

None of the other guests was into fly-fishing. Neither was Tony Gonzales. Saltwater fly-fishing was still in its infancy or, perhaps, its adolescence in those days. Joe Brooks and Jimmy Albright and Ted Williams and a lot of other great anglers had shown what could be done down in the Florida Keys, and the sport was growing slowly. But it was still a pretty rarefied kind of angling, where you had to stalk fish very carefully and then make long accurate casts, frequently in windy conditions. You had to be a very good caster and use a technique called "double hauling," which took some practice to get the timing down, like double-clutching a car. But once you'd mastered it—and back then, few anglers had—you could cast a very long line.

The first morning we were at Boca Paila, Ralph and I went out on the flat and caught a lot of bonefish on a fly—more bonefish, in one morning, than I'd caught in my life up until then. It was, by far, the best fishing I'd ever had in salt water. And it got better.

Tony Gonzales watched what we were doing, and he was fascinated. And, maybe, he saw the shape of things to come. At any rate, he wanted to learn how to fly-fish, and he was a quick learner. He had the mechanics down and was making good casts in fifteen minutes. After two days, he was double hauling like an expert and laying out long, straight casts.

In the afternoon, we were back out on the flats, and I caught the first permit of my life. The permit is a sort of moon-shaped fish, with a large, black scythe of a tail that sticks up out of the water when it is feeding on shallow flats. It is very wary and a terrific fighter. It is rare and hard to fool with a fly, and back then, a permit of any size, taken on a fly, was considered the fish of a lifetime. Of the three species of flats fish—bonefish, tarpon, and permit—the permit is clearly the most difficult to find and catch. Some of the best of the Florida Keys anglers had never had a chance at one. Before Joe Brooks became the first angler to land a permit on a fly rod, many anglers thought it might not ever be done. (Joe, I might add, used an Orvis impregnated bamboo rod to accomplish that feat.)

Now, on my first day at this wonderful new, remote camp, I had landed a permit; we had found paradise.

And, then, a little while later we spotted another permit, and I caught that one, too. We caught two more permit as well as a few small tarpon before we left. I wrote in the *Orvis News* that we had discovered "the ultimate in saltwater fly-fishing."

I was so enthusiastic about that place—and about the possibilities of exotic travel in general—that I quickly got Orvis into the travel business. We formed something called the Big Ten Club, which was a sort of destinations wish list, and when we wrote up a new destination in the *News,* we told the readers to give us a call and we'd book their trip for them. I hired someone to take care of it, and it seemed like a natural fit. But there was a lot more to it, which I learned later. Orvis came out sadder and wiser and lucky that it wasn't worse.

Meanwhile, I continued to travel and scout out these wonderful new destinations, usually with my boys. Shortly after the Boca Paila trip, Ralph, Perk, Dave—my youngest, who was eleven at the time—and I took a trip to Alaska, north of Dillingham. We stayed at Tikchick Lodge, which had just opened. A man named Bob Curtis was the proprietor, and he was a real Alaskan figure, a wild and woolly bush pilot and adventurer who knew the country and was a good host. The fishing around the lodge was wonderful, and every day we would fly out to a new river and catch rainbow trout, sockeye salmon, arctic char, and grayling on dry flies.

After a few days of watching us, Bob decided we were reasonably competent, so he suggested we make a float trip down the Nusgogak River. We were game, so he flew us out with one canoe, one river raft, a couple of tents, and some cooking gear. We were at the confluence of the King Salmon and Nusgogak Rivers, about as high in the system as he could get his Helio-Courier float plane in. It was extremely remote country, and I was a little apprehensive. We didn't even have a map.

Bob put us out on a beach and said he would come back for us in three to five days. If the weather was clear enough.

"How will you find us?" I asked him.

He just said, "I'll find you." His confidence was persuasive, but I should have been a lot more apprehensive. My boys and I had done a lot of canoeing and camping, but we'd never been anyplace as wild and remote as this.

The boys were unconcerned so we divided the load and started downstream in the raft and canoe, fishing along the way.

On the evening of our first day, the fishing was slow, and we decided to camp where we found a nice stream coming into the river from the east. We thought there would be enough breeze to keep the mosquitoes—which were as big and hungry as advertised—down a little.

As soon as we started fishing, we realized we had picked the perfect spot. We were catching two- and three-pound rainbow and char on just about every cast. We had unloaded the raft and the canoe but hadn't set up camp yet, since the fishing was so good and we had plenty of light in Alaska in the summer. Then, from upstream and across the river, we heard a rather loud, menacing noise. We all turned at once and saw a mammoth brown bear standing on her hind legs, looking about twelve feet tall, with a couple of cubs close at her side.

Ralph and Dave kept fishing. Perk put his rod down and started loading our gear back on the raft and the canoe. He wasn't taking his time, either.

I said I didn't think the bears looked very hostile, and, besides, the fishing was awfully good. Ralph and Dave backed me up. Ralph, who was the Alaskan guide of the family, used the word "chicken," but Perk said he had a better word and that was "brains." He then pointed out that he was the only one among us who had ever made the honor roll in school, and *he* thought we ought to get the hell out of there.

The majority finally prevailed, even though we had a minority of good sense on that trip. That night, after we had set up camp, cooked, eaten dinner, and gone to bed, it became apparent that the bears, if not hostile, were certainly very curious and had come over to examine our camp site at closer range. They weren't particularly hungry, as the salmon were running and they had plenty of their natural food, but they did get close enough that Ralph, Dave, and I began to think that we should have paid more attention to Perk. It was not a restful night.

The next couple of days were eventful but not dangerous. We caught fish, saw more bears, and came across the largest moose I have ever seen. He was standing serenely in the middle of the river, and we had to decide whether to go in front of him, behind him, or even under him. Perk, who had some credibility by now, said we should go behind him, which we did.

The third day turned out to be a near disaster.

Ralph and I were in the canoe. Perk and Dave, in the rubber raft, were ahead of us a little, and when we came to an island in the river, they took one side and we took the other. It turned out to be a very big island, and when we got to what we thought would be the end of it, we found another fork and, farther down, yet another. I realized we were in some sort of delta, and I had no idea when the river would come back into a single stream again. The younger boys had all the food in their boat. We had the camping gear in our canoe. Ralph and I figured the only thing to do was paddle fast and every time we came to the point of an island, make a mark showing which side we'd taken. The canoe was a good deal faster than the raft, so there was a possibility that Perk and Dave might recognize our marks as they came along behind us. But I was, needless to say, very concerned.

After about two hours, we got back together by sheer chance and good luck. Perk and Dave hadn't been concerned, nor had they seen any of the makeshift signs we'd left. Later, when I looked at a map of the area, it seemed impossible that we should ever have found each other. The river had multiple channels for about fifteen miles of its length.

It was a great trip, then, with good fishing, lots of adventures, and even a close call. Ralph was so taken with Alaska that he stayed on and worked as a guide for Bob Curtis for the rest of the summer. That had been our third trip to Alaska together. I had no way of knowing that it would be our last.

The next summer, in July 1969, I continued to broaden my sporting travel. I took my mother, who had been my first fishing companion, to the most famous Atlantic salmon river—for big fish—in the world, the Alta, in Norway. It was a chance for me to pay her back, just a little, for all the memorable fishing trips she had taken me on. Not just anybody gets to fish the Alta, and those who do are willing to pay dearly for the privilege. But I was able to get on at a bargain price because of the Orvis travel business.

So it was a special trip, and we were both excited about the prospects. The Alta is above the Arctic Circle, in rough country. It is a big river—too big to wade—so you fish from a very large canoelike craft some twenty-eight feet long. You do not anchor, the way you do in Canada, but trawl with the guide rowing for control and slowly losing ground to the current, swinging the stern of the boat from one side to the other to position the angler, who doesn't even cast, really, just holds his rod and leaves some line in the water and lets the boat position the fly. Not my idea of a particularly interesting way to fish, and I got into trouble with the guides right away.

They wanted us to use the fifteen- and sixteen-foot, Norwegian two-handed rods, which were traditional. I said I would stick with my nine-and-a-half and ten-foot Orvis impregnated bamboo rods, which you cast with one hand. Since I was paying, that seemed my prerogative.

Well, I missed three fish, two of which struck short of the fly, so it didn't have anything to do with the rod. But the autocratic gillie—which is what the guides are called—took my rod away from me, gave me one of the long, two-handed jobs, and said, "Now you will fish with this rod."

I was furious, and I said, "No, I won't."

Well, my own mother went along with the guide, and even though it was my trip and I was paying, I found myself being put ashore, almost as though by a mutinous crew.

It was very humiliating, but I knew exactly what was in Mother's mind. She had come a long way to catch a big Alta River salmon, and she knew how much that depended on the guide. If your guide doesn't like you, he can make damn sure you don't catch a fish. Mother figured with me out of the boat, she'd go along with the guide and have a lot better chance at a fish. The injury to her own son's pride was a small price to pay. That's what angling fever does to people. Especially when you're talking Atlantic salmon.

The way it turned out, Mother did catch a fish, and I got very, very cold trying to fish that huge river without waders. I managed to catch three juvenile salmon (called grilse), but the real accomplishment was that I managed not to drown myself.

It was a lousy start to the trip.

It never gets dark in those latitudes at that time of year, so you fish from seven in the evening until four in the morning, when the routine is for the sports to sit around a table drinking from a bottle of whiskey—which they provide. The gillies sit around another table drinking from a bottle that has also been provided by the sports. The gillies generally finished their bottle first, and when this happened, one of them would walk over to the sports' table and pick up their bottle and take it back to the gillies' table.

My regard for the gillies, as you can tell, was not exactly high. And I wasn't shy about letting it show. So Mother took me aside, just like I was ten years old, and told me to adjust my attitude, or we wouldn't catch any fish. So much for being the big shot and the host.

I never used the long Norwegian rods, but otherwise I did what I was told, and it worked. We caught fish. None of ours was over twenty-two pounds, but one member of our party caught one that weighed forty-six pounds. When he flew back to Michigan, he carried the fish with him on his lap.

Mother and I went to another river, the Flam, after the Alta, and while I was there I got a phone call from the States with news of the greatest tragedy of my life. My son Ralph had drowned at the age of eighteen. After a heavy rain, his mother had asked him to go remove a screen from the culvert outlet of a pond. Ralph apparently slipped and was sucked into the culvert and lodged there.

I hope I never have to tell that story again.

I think of Ralph all the time, and all my thoughts involve happy memories, like those trips to Alaska. As I write this, my youngest daughter, Melissa, has just named her third child Ralph. He is a sturdy, happy baby, and I couldn't be more pleased.

Chapter 8

New Beginnings

The year 1969 produced both the blackest and the brightest days of my life. A few months after losing my son Ralph, I married again. Romi and I are still together almost thirty years later, which is proof of her patience and stamina and—one more time— my good luck. She is the most beautiful and exciting person I have ever met. She always knows what needs to be done, and she does it. She has great energy, impeccable taste, and she does not cut corners. Before she met me, her idea of fun in the outdoors was tennis followed by a dip in the pool. But to my delight, she has taken up my sports of fly-fishing and bird hunting, and, being the perfectionist that she is, she has become excellent at both. I have to admit I haven't reciprocated as much as I should have. I am a lousy tennis player, and I don't enjoy art museums or symphony orchestras. But Romi has managed to get me to listen to classical music instead of country-western, and I suppose in another thirty years, I will be even more civilized and refined.

Romi and I got started almost right away on the traveling. One of our first trips was to Belize, and it was a great success. So much so that a few years later, when I got a letter from a young man named Vic Barothy, Jr., inviting me down to fish off his houseboat, I decided to try it again.

I didn't know the young man personally, but the name certainly got my attention. Vic Barothy, Sr.—his late father—had a well-deserved reputation for running trips where you lived on a houseboat and fished out of skiffs for tarpon and bonefish, using light tackle. Those kinds of expeditions take a lot of logistical ability and angling competence, and the number of things that can go wrong is just about endless. But Barothy was a master, the top name in the business. He was a guy with a lot of ability who came out of Michigan and learned the business in the Florida Keys before he went over to Cuba and set up a first-rate outfitting business.

When Castro took over in Cuba, Vic got out with just the clothes on his back and made it to the United States, but some of his captains later took off in his boats and made it down to Belize, which was then British Honduras. They got in touch with Vic, who was in Florida, and said, "Boss, come on down, we've got your boats, and we're ready to go to work." Vic joined his old captains and set up two very well-regarded fishing camps.

Well, Vic Jr. must have been a son from very late in the old man's life. When he wrote to Orvis, I recognized the name, and I thought it would be a great opportunity to get away with Romi and our youngest daughter, Melissa, and also do a little exploration for the travel business. If the trip was any good, I'd write it up in the *News* and add it to our list of destinations.

It turned out to be a wonderful trip. Young Barothy had obviously inherited his father's love of sport fishing. He knew the reefs, and he was handy around boats. He put on a great show with a very good mate and good food and excellent fishing on the flats for bonefish and permit. We also went up in the mangrove rivers, which were beautiful, but the fishing wasn't very good because they had been fished very hard by the Carribs, seminomadic people who virtually live out of boats. But it was great sight-seeing and a wonderful time together, and, while we were disappointed when a storm came up and cut our trip short by a few days, I went back to work feeling like I could recommend the trip, without qualification, to our customers.

So I didn't hold back when I wrote my story. "Vic Barothy Jr.'s operation," I enthused, "is a conspicuous case of success . . . an owner, operator doing what he knows best and what he thoroughly enjoys."

If the trip had gone on a little longer—or if I had just realized that the young man was certainly going to put on his best performance for the boss of Orvis and his wife—then I might not have written with quite so much enthusiasm. But we published the story in the *News,* and within weeks young Barothy was booked solid for a year.

Well, it turned out that he didn't have the experience or the infrastructure to handle that kind of business, and pretty soon we started getting complaints from customers about how he would take them out and then run out of gas, or food, or water, or the boat would break down, until, eventually, he just didn't show up for one party, and the people had to get on the plane and go on home.

This was not what we had in mind for the Orvis customer, needless to say, when we started booking trips through the *Orvis News;* and in truth, I don't blame the young man as much as I blame myself. You can't generalize from one trip, the way I did, and I should have been aware of the complexity and difficulty involved in putting on trips of that kind on a regular basis out of a place as remote as Belize.

And that wasn't the only trip where we had problems. We were also sending customers down to Boca Paila, where I'd had such a good experience with the bonefish and permit. One party—an elderly couple, dropped at the little landing strip where there was no shelter and no sign of human life, nothing except some Mayan ruins off in the jungle a little way, which weren't too reassuring—found themselves abandoned there. When the plane that had brought them in flew off, there was no sign of anyone to meet them. They waited. And they waited. And the longer they waited there in the hot sun, the more uncomfortable and concerned they got until they were pretty sure they were going to perish there on the side of that airstrip.

Finally, after about four hours, someone came to get them. When they got back, they let us know what had happened. They could have been a lot tougher on us than they were. We apologized and sent them gift certificates, and, at the urging of my board of directors, Orvis got out of the travel business. I was reluctant because I thought that, more and more, sportsmen were going to be on the lookout for remote destinations where the fishing or hunting would be wild and unspoiled. But as my board pointed out, we weren't making much money in the travel business, we were making more customers unhappy than happy with Orvis, and, the way things were going, we were running the risk of losing a lot of money in a big lawsuit.

So I gave in. Orvis stopped booking trips. But that didn't mean *I* stopped making them.

I should say a word or two about my board of directors since it is unusual for a privately held corporation to have a board; traditionally, the board represents the interests of the stockholders in its relations with management—including the hiring and firing of the chief executive officer. In the case of Orvis, the stock was not merely held privately, it was held by myself and my children and grandchildren, and I was management. So what role was there for a board?

Well, I have always profited from good advice and wise counsel. My experience in getting separated from Harris Calorific proved to me that the advice of someone who is more experienced than you, and smarter than you, and who has a little distance on the problem, can be invaluable. John Drinko had given me some very good advice, and, because I had taken it, I now had my own company to run. But just because I was now the boss, that didn't mean I was suddenly going to have all the answers. Good advice would probably be more important than ever, and, frankly, in Manchester, Vermont, I wasn't really sure where I would go to get it. The local bankers and businessmen were fine fellows, and, in fact, Duckie Corkran had a board that consisted of some of those men. But I had bigger things in mind.

I put together a board of people who had broad experience and whose judgment I respected. Originally, most of them were from Cleveland. John Drinko was on the board, and so was the president of John's company, Cleveland Institute of Electronics, Branco Pfeiffer. He was a computer genius, which was a real asset for Orvis later on. There was also Dick Whitney, who was in the chemical business in Cleveland; Al Whitehouse, CEO of Standard Oil of Ohio; and Jerry Tone, vice president of sales for a fiberglass tank company. And later there was Bob Mitchell, vice chairman of Celanese Corporation, plus Don Kendall, retired CEO of Pepsico, and Joe Williams, CEO of the Williams Group.

The purpose of my board then and now has been to serve as advisers. It exists, mainly, to curb my enthusiasms. And over the years, I have to say, I have gotten some very sound advice from my board. I probably would have hung in there with the travel business, for instance, if it hadn't been for the unanimous opinion of the board that we should get out. The travel business, I now understand, calls for very close attention to detail. People who spend a lot of money to go to some exotic destination expect a high level of service, and we were simply too small, and growing in too many other directions at the time, to give it the kind of attention that it needed. I'm glad I had the board there to give me that advice at the time, and I'm glad that I took it. I might add that now that Orvis is a much bigger company and able to recruit from a much larger talent pool, it is getting back into the travel business. That's one of many good decisions my sons Perk (the new CEO) and Dave have made. Dave will be in charge of the new Orvis Travel, and I expect he'll put together the staff and the systems to do a lot better in the travel business than I did.

Another example of my board giving me the advice I needed when I needed it came in the early seventies, when the company was growing very fast and we found ourselves with surplus cash. I thought this was a good opportunity for us to get into some new things, so I came up with a shopping list of new product lines and marketing programs I thought we should consider. Al Whitehouse cautioned me. He said, and the board agreed, that you should never go into something because of a cash push. It was crucial to have an idea pull—if the idea was good enough, the cash could be found. That was very good advice. I took it and dropped all of the suggestions on my shopping list.

There have been other examples, over the years, and I would say that there has never been a case where the board and I were at serious odds over an important issue for the company. We've never had anyone resign in protest over some company policy. I've been fortunate to have the board. But you might wonder what's in it for them. We don't pay the members of my board very much, as those things are measured. And we couldn't pay the kind of people I've got on my board the kind of money that would persuade them to take on the job unless they wanted to do it anyway. Don Kendall, who was the CEO of Pepsico, isn't going to be influenced by the size of his Orvis director's fee.

So we give them something that is in the Orvis spirit. During the summer, we have our board meeting in Wyoming, and we fish for trout on the spring creeks out there. In the fall, we meet in Cleveland, and we go duck shooting on a marsh that belongs to one of the great old duck clubs there, thanks to our directors Dick Whitney and Al Whitehouse, who are members. The winter meeting is at my place down in Florida, where we do some quail hunting. And the spring meeting is either in Vermont—for turkey hunting and trout fishing—or in England, where we fish the classic chalk streams, the Test and the Itchen.

So the meetings are not what you'd call a hardship. A big improvement, I'd say, over a corporate boardroom, which is something these guys have seen plenty of. In fact, I have a lot of people asking me how they can get on the board. And one of the people who is already on it said to me once, "You know, Leigh, I think you could get some of those people to pay *you* to be on the board."

Interestingly, I get a lot of women volunteers, but what I tell them is that I already have an overload of advice from women friends for free.

* * *

From the time I bought Orvis, the company grew at a fairly dramatic pace. We were at a half million in 1965, when I took over. In 1970, we were five times that big. By 1975, ten years after I bought Orvis, it was at six million, net sales, and two years after that it was well over ten million.

I cite these figures to point out that Orvis was in a very dynamic situation, almost from the start. Some of this was because leisure time activity was growing, and some of it was because we had found our niche and our image and were doing a good job of finding our customers and giving them what they wanted. And some of the growth was due to factors that were way beyond our control or anyone else's. This was a time when the way people shopped was changing. Mail-order marketing was coming into its own, and, more and more, people were shopping by catalog. We had gone from sending out a few thousand catalogs twice a year to sending out millions four or five times a year.

And, gradually, as we sent out more catalogs, more people began calling in their orders. The number of phone orders increased as people became accustomed to paying by credit card. The big breakthrough, in this regard, came when we could accept credit-card billings over the phone without signatures. This was a real departure, and when it took hold, mail order was really on its way. And then the overnight mail services came into their own, so people could order something today and expect delivery the day after tomorrow. When I am at my place out in Grover, Wyoming, I can call in an order before one P.M. today and receive, say, a new pair of waders before one P.M. tomorrow, well in time for the evening hatch. All this cut through the greatest drawback to mail-order shopping, which was that most people want instant gratification and aren't willing to wait for a week or ten days after they've made up their minds they want something and are willing to pay for it. They want it right away. Now you didn't have to fill out any orders, write any checks, or lick any stamps. You just picked up the phone and made a call. It moved mail-order shopping a lot closer to the kind of impulse buying you see people doing at the mall. And finally, there was a large cultural change that worked to the advantage of mail order. More and more women were working and no longer had the time to shop. Women are much better mail-order shoppers than men and soon accounted for a very large percentage of the business.

All this meant that we were growing rapidly. Growth can be a challenge, all by itself, but the way we were growing threw some additional challenges our way and required some new ways of doing things at our end. We had to hire people and come up with systems to handle the tremendous new volume, and, of course, in the middle of all of this, we got the computer, which is what really made it all possible. But in the early days, computers not only solved problems, they created challenges, especially when it came to training.

I came along before computers, so I didn't really understand them and still don't. But I understood, from my contacts with other people in the mail-order business, that life was not going to be possible without computers. So with the valuable help and advice of Branco Pfeiffer, who was on my board, I started hiring people who did understand computers, and they began designing new systems to take care of fulfillment and inventory control. For the better part of a decade, we were—like everybody else in the indus-try—fighting to stay ahead of the curve. It was a situation where what is state of the art today is obsolete tomorrow. The company was growing rapidly and changing profoundly at the same time.

Some of those changes took place within what had always been the core of our business—fly-fishing.

When I took over the business, one of my goals was eventu-ally to sell a complete line of Orvis fly-fishing products. At the time, the Orvis company sold reels made by Hardy of England to go with our rods, and it was a good fit. I'm sure we were, by far, Hardy's largest customer in the United States. But not a very exclusive customer, because they sold to Abercrombie & Fitch as well as to many smaller outlets. In about 1970, Jim Hardy—the director of sales—came over from England to "advise" us that the Hardy com-pany would no longer be supplying the United States with their lightweight series of reels. Hardy had made an arrangement with another company—Scientific Anglers—to develop a new line of reels to be distributed exclusively in the United States. We were told that we would be supplied with these reels from Scientific Anglers.

Well, I was more than a little incensed. I didn't like being told what products I would, and would not, offer my customers, and I had no desire to play second fiddle to Scientific Anglers or anyone else. I made the firm decision, then and there, to sell and promote only Orvis-branded products in the very near future.

Right away, I made an arrangement with another British fly-reel manufacturer to produce a lightweight reel similar to the Hardy, which we would sell as the Orvis Battenkill. The reel was a success in spite of some quality problems. I suppose that is understandable when you consider the following story.

I had made a date to visit the new managing director of the reel company to talk about our contract and to go over quality and delivery problems. We had a nice talk in his office for an hour or so, and after receiving assurances that all of our problems would be taken care of, I asked to visit the factory. The managing director was appalled. Why in God's name would I want to visit the factory? I then learned that the managing director had never been in the factory himself. In fact, he couldn't even find his way there.

I did visit the factory and found that they had some good mechanics working there, but they had no budget for maintenance and updating of machinery. Unlike the managing director, I knew a little something about the way things worked in a factory, and I knew that we needed a different source for reels. I figured that in order to have our own true proprietary product, we'd need to start from scratch, beginning with the design. So I contacted Stan Bogden, whose reels were highly prized by American salmon fishermen, and commissioned him to design an aesthetically pleasing, lightweight fly reel with no concern for cost.

I wanted a good reel that looked handsome, sounded good (fly fisherman like a solid clicking sound from a fly reel), performed well, and didn't cost a fortune. I insisted that we be able to deliver it when we said we would. When Bogden delivered his prototype, I had our engineering people alter it to make it more economical and then put it out on bid for production. Hardy was low bidder and manufactured the reel exclusively for us, according to our design and using Orvis tooling. We called it the CFO, in honor of Charles F. Orvis. It is still the quality reel that sets the standards for aesthetics, light weight, and acoustical delight in fly-fishing. The decision to sell only Orvis-branded products paid off, and not only in terms of sheer pride. In the manufacturing and marketing of fly reels—a product we didn't even make when I came aboard— Orvis is number one in the world today.

Even when you are growing in new areas, you have to pay attention to your core business because there will be changes there too. One of the lessons you learn in any business is that things change whether you want them to or not. You might be perfectly happy to go on doing things the way you've always done them, but the technology changes or the market changes and you have two choices— you can either change, too, and survive and maybe even grow, or you can keep on doing things the way you've always done them and die.

At Orvis, the flagship product, not just in terms of the revenue it produced but also in terms of the company's image, was the impregnated bamboo fly rod. Because we'd had such difficulty finding reliable supplies of bamboo, we tried substitutes. I wanted to make sure we would still be able to sell quality rods, no matter what happened in China.

Glass rods had been around a long time. I'd had a good experience, down in Cuba, with one my brother had given me. And other companies—especially Fenwick—were doing a good business with their glass fly rods. We had our own glass rod, and it was a good product. Glass rods were lighter than bamboo and could be made with a good deal of uniformity. Good glass rods were better than mediocre bamboo rods. But glass didn't have the rate of recovery or the resilience of bamboo and took a set more readily. Orvis was only interested in making the best, so our glass rods were almost a sideline that we offered to our budget-conscious customers. Primarily, we made impregnated bamboo rods, which were superior, and we dominated that market. If we couldn't make bamboo rods, we were going to have to find a new material for making a superior fly rod, or we might not be making anything at all.

In 1972, on one of my trips to England, I was talking to Bill Hardy, who was president of the Hardy company, which was now making the CFO for Orvis. Hardy had gotten out of bamboo and gone completely to glass for rod making, which seemed like a bad decision to me, for the same reason it would have been bad for Orvis. Their rods were price competitive with Fenwick but not as good.

Bill said they had looked at another material, a space-age synthetic, called carbon fiber in the U.K. and graphite in the United States. "It looked promising," Bill said, and showed me some samples that he had on his desk, "but we decided not to pursue it."

When I left his office, I had other ideas for Orvis.

Back in Vermont, I told Howard Steere, the Orvis plant manager, that we ought to look into this material. We were still having trouble acquiring enough bamboo, of the right quality, to fulfill our demand. There were times when we were down to thirty twelve-foot poles to make rods. And, then, there were other times when we had ten thousand. But we were growing very rapidly and so was the demand for our rods, and I was concerned about keeping up.

Once we started working with graphite, we discovered that it was potentially superior to bamboo. And we now realized that we had competitors in this new technology that would very likely replace our bamboo fly rod. So we could not afford to ignore graphite even if the bamboo supply problems eased up. In other words, we were jumping into graphite rod production with both feet even before we knew for sure that quality, durable, graphite rods could be made. But the alternative, pretty clearly, was to shrink and, maybe, to die.

With the approval of the board, I gave Howard the green light on building a new rod factory and on acquiring the tooling and technology to get into graphite and do it right. When I discussed this with my board, Bob Mitchell said, "Well, have you talked to my people about it?" Bob was vice president of the Celanese Corporation. One of its subdivisions, Narmco Materials, had been doing some research into graphite and had developed something called low-modulus graphite. In nontechnical language, this graphite didn't break like the other stuff. We tested it, and we were so pleased with it that we went right into production. We came out with our graphite rods about six months after Fenwick and Shakespeare came out with theirs. But we had far less breakage, and our rods were an immediate success with our customers.

Graphite turned out to be an ideal material for fly-rod building. It is much lighter than bamboo or glass, has a much higher rate of recovery than either, and has an infinitesimal rate of fatigue. When Orvis found a way to overcome the breakage problem and developed the right tapers to take advantage of this new material, we had the game won. Incidentally, the two rod makers— Shakespeare and Fenwick—that beat us to the market are no longer significant competitors.

Even though there was some initial skepticism among old-line anglers, the graphite technology took over fly-fishing. We were there from the beginning, and we are still the industry leader. After we had started selling our graphite rods, I was back in England and having lunch with a man named Jim Miller, who was chairman of Hardy's parent company. Jim was a keen angler, and I asked him what he thought of graphite. He said, "There's nothing to it. Glass is good enough for the trout angler, and the salmon anglers will always insist on cane." I thought to myself that this was the kind of competitor I liked. It turned out that while most salmon anglers were wealthy, they were also relatively old, and when they learned that graphite rods weigh less than half of what bamboo salmon rods did, and took much less effort to cast (giving an angler additional years to fish), they switched.

We still make bamboo rods for the traditionalist, and we sell a few hundred every year. But graphite is far and away the industry standard and where the action is. The graphite story is another case where my board was a real asset. And it is also a great credit to Howard Steere, who was a brilliant and inventive mechanic and also a frugal Maine Yankee, who did what needed to be done without going over budget. It isn't often that you move into something that is a totally new product, made out of a totally new material, requiring completely new tooling, and do it without having to make major corrections along the way. Also, it isn't often that you come out with something that is a hit right from the beginning. Howard's first two rods, which we called the Far and Fine and the eight-foot, six-weight Trout Rod, are still in the catalog and still selling today.

Building rods, of course, was our business and always had been. We knew something about building quality fly rods. In fact, we knew a lot about it. We had more experience in that field than any of our competitors, I think it is fair to say. But at about the time we were moving into graphite and becoming a much bigger player, we were also getting into something that had not traditionally been the Orvis business and which we didn't know anything about. It was a new world for us, and it turned out to be our greatest area of growth.

I'm talking about women's clothes.

Orvis had always had a few items of women's apparel, going back to Duckie's time. His wife, Skippie, persuaded him to put a few things for women in the store so that when the men came in to shop for fishing tackle, their wives would be able to find something they could buy and not be trying to drag their husbands out of the store. But there wasn't much, and it wasn't available in a wide selection of styles or sizes. This is the tough thing about any kind of clothing, but especially women's clothing. You have to be big enough that you can afford to carry a large inventory, and for a long time, we weren't.

We also didn't know anything about that business, and we had a lot going on, and a lot of growth, in the things we did know about. But as we got bigger, it became harder and harder to ignore

women's clothing, even if I didn't know anything about it. You
didn't have to be a mail-order genius to see that there was a lot of
action there. Everybody was coming out with catalogs for the prep-
pie look. And you didn't necessarily need to have your roots in the
women's apparel business to succeed there. Lands' End had been
in the business of selling sailing hardware before it discovered soft
goods. Carroll Reed went from being a ski shop to a lady's clothing
catalog. So it wasn't so much of a reach for Orvis, which was selling a way of living, to include some women's clothing along with
the highball glasses and the framed prints and the other products
that suggested country elegance.

We knew that much, anyway; but we didn't know much more
than that. There weren't many people in the world less qualified
than I was to go out and start putting together a line of women's
clothing. I needed talent for that, and, fortunately, I found it in house.

Actually, I shouldn't have been at all surprised by this since
it was shortly after I started running Orvis that I realized we had
some incredibly bright and able women working for us. They were
the "can do, will do, and here is a better way" sort of people you
need in any successful business. While I was coming from a background in the mines and the welding business, where there weren't
many women on the job, I couldn't miss that this wasn't the case
at Orvis. I finally came to the conclusion that there were limited
job opportunities in our little community and that the women
were more likely to stick with us than the men, who moved on to
other places, while the women stayed on and made a difference.

One of our buyers, Nancy Aiken, was from Westchester County.
She and her husband had a ski place in Vermont, and, like a lot of
people, she wanted to spend more time there, so she took a job at
Orvis. She bought fishhooks and things like that back in the days
before computers when the system was to go through the ware-
house and look at the bins. When you saw one that was nearly
empty, you reordered.

Well, Nancy Aiken had talent and good taste—she was the
typical Orvis customer as well as being an employee—and she had

a lot of drive. When I said I thought we needed to get some women's clothing into the catalog, she convinced me that she could design and develop a line of clothing that would fit right in with the Orvis image.

She started bringing in things like cashmere sweaters, loden capes, and tweed jackets and skirts. Everything was natural fibers and of a classic look. And the clothing Nancy developed was an immediate hit. She had a good eye, and she knew what worked for Orvis. I couldn't help her at all. I was always happy to go down and talk to Howard Steere at the rod shop and put in my two bits' worth, but I didn't have anything to contribute to the women's clothing decisions. Every now and then Romi would give me an idea, and I'd pass it along.

Occasionally, I'd veto something because I didn't think it was right for the Orvis image. We'd always had a lot of dog images— especially of Labs—on things like glasses and rugs. I like dogs, and I thought those products worked fine. Nancy thought we should also have things with cat images because there were a lot more people out there with cats than there were with dogs. But I said no. I've never liked cats. Then one year she designed this sweatshirt with an image on the front of a cat watching a mousehole. On the back there was an image of the mice inside the mousehole, and they were having a party. Well, I vetoed it. But she politely explained that while I might be the boss, in this case I was wrong, and she put the sweatshirt in anyway. That sweatshirt was a big success, so we now have cats—as well as dogs— in the catalog.

As the women's clothing division got bigger and bigger, we got flak from some of our old fishing customers, who wanted to know what ladies' clothes were doing in *their* catalog. But not enough to make me take them out. We kept adding more and more and selling more and more until, pretty soon, the tail was wagging the dog, and we were doing a lot more of our mail-order volume in women's clothing than we were in hunting and fishing. (Hunting and fishing—along with other, related "hard" goods—does better in the stores and is more profitable overall.) We've had people—consultants and new employees—tell us that what we really need to do is get out of hunting and fishing, where the growth has not been as dramatic and the market is much smaller, and concentrate on women's clothing. But, of course, there is no chance of that. The Orvis identity is a big part of what moves those clothes, and that identity is in the sporting life. We did, however, split off the catalogs in the late eighties, so that people who buy only the hunting and fishing products get that catalog. And we have catalogs for gifts and travel, clothes, home furnishings—five catalogs in all. But women's clothing still accounts for a majority of the mail-order volume.

Chapter 9

The Customer Is Always Right . . .
Even When You Know
Damned Well He's Wrong

S ometime in the late seventies or early eighties, I was having a conversation with a few of the key people in the company. We were growing at a very nice rate—by 1980 we were at nineteen million in sales and had years when we increased sales as much as 65 percent. Orvis was already bigger than I had ever expected it would be, and there was no end in sight. I remember reading in his biography that Sam Walton—who is one of my heroes—was asked by a reporter, way back before he'd even opened his first Wal-Mart, when he had just a few Ben Franklin stores, how much bigger he thought his company would get. Sam said he thought he was about as big as he would ever get, right then, so you never know.

The only thing I knew, back when I bought the company, was that I wanted it to grow. I didn't necessarily know how big. I do remember saying that when the company got to six million, I was going to buy an airplane. I said that in my first year with Orvis. We're over two hundred million now, and we still don't have that airplane.

So growth is not something you can predict. But you can manage it—you'd better manage it, or you'll get in trouble. At that meeting with those key people, somebody made the point that, while we were growing pretty quickly, we could do a lot more simply by mailing out more catalogs, or by putting more pages into those we were already sending out. Within limits, there was an almost direct correlation.

It seemed like an obvious call. Every business wants to get bigger and make more money. But I said no.

Later on, Tom Vaccaro—who was CFO then and is now—told me he thought that was one of the best decisions I'd ever made. (In Tom's opinion, the very best decision I ever made was to go out and convince our competitors that we ought to trade lists, and I'll have to agree with him there.)

It *was* a good decision to not push for more growth at that time. It was the right decision for a very simple reason: we could have forced the additional growth, but we didn't have the people or the system or the suppliers to handle it. And that is how I explained the decision to the people at that meeting. If we had gone ahead and sent out more catalogs and pushed for the extra growth, we would have had a tough time getting in the inventory and handling the additional orders. There would have been a lot of disappointed customers. Orders would have been delayed. Items would have been out of stock. All of the nightmares on the fulfillment side of the equation would have come true.

I believe very strongly that in mail order, your customer doesn't remember the quality of product nearly as well as he remembers the quality of service. In those days when mail order was growing so rapidly, a lot of companies got into trouble when they couldn't keep up on the fulfillment side of the equation. One of my firm goals has always been that, after a transaction with Orvis, the customer should go away with a positive feeling about the company—whether he was ordering something, returning something, or just asking a question. Customers often forget about product—good or bad—but they never forget about service, especially bad.

I tell Orvis employees, and it is posted on the walls around the office, "The customer is always right. Even when you know damned well he's wrong."

Over the years, this attitude led us to develop a relationship with a lot of customers that went beyond the usual, arm's-length kind of dealing. We encouraged this, of course, through the *News* and the schools. We wanted people to think of us as more than just a supplier of the hard goods they needed to live the sporting life. Orvis was where they had learned to fly-fish, and where, a few years later, they sent the picture of the big trout they caught on an Orvis rod.

This resulted in some interesting stories along the way, where we found ourselves dealing with people as if they were friends— or even family—and not just customers. I remember one early episode when a woman wrote me a personal letter asking me if I would use my influence at Orvis to get her husband's picture—with his trophy fish—into the *Orvis News*. She went on to say that her husband was a prominent businessman and had sent the picture in some time back. Now, every time he received his *News* and saw that his picture hadn't been published, he turned very grumpy. She closed by saying that, while her husband might not be as handsome as Lee Wulff, the famous angler, she thought he looked pretty good, and he was *really* proud of that fish.

I wrote her right back and apologized, saying that it had been a grievous mistake not to publish the picture and that we would do so in the next issue. I enclosed the man's Record Catch pin and said that I thought he deserved the pin primarily for capturing such a kind and thoughtful wife.

We frequently got letters from people who were dissatisfied, for one reason or another, and had taken the time to write in a thoughtful way, and many of those letters led to rather interesting correspondences. I still remember the letter I got from a customer who said he had just received a pair of binoculars that he'd ordered from us. "I do not understand them," the man wrote. "They do not magnify or bring distant objects closer, they make all objects appear farther away in the distance. Is this the way they should be, or am I using them incorrectly?"

We all imagined the man sitting there believing that Orvis had somehow put the damned glasses together *backwards*. Then we wrote the man back, suggesting that maybe he was looking through the wrong end of the binoculars and that if he turned them around he might get better performance.

I got a letter once from a doctor in Georgia who had gone off to Quebec on a fishing trip with a brand-new pair of wading shoes that he had ordered from Orvis.

"When I got to L'Etape," he wrote, "I put on my waders and then discovered that what I thought was a pair of shoes turned out to be two left shoes. I admit that sometimes when I wade in strange water, I am a bit clumsy, but I did not realize that the Orvis people thought of me as having two left feet. So, look carefully on the shelf for those two right shoes, size 13, and send one down to me along with any words of consolation that you can muster. I will return one of the most traveled wading shoes in the history of your company."

I wrote him back:

"I don't know how to begin to apologize for the two left shoes. You seem extremely patient and fortunately have a sense of humor. Needless to say, a right and a left pair will be on their way to you immediately.

"I find this situation particularly ironic and embarrassing as a number of years ago, my brother showed up as my guest at a duck marsh with a pair of Sears & Roebuck rubber boots. He proceeded to show his disloyalty, ungraciousness, and bad manners by pointing out to a group of duck hunters what a helluva bargain he had gotten and how much better off he was shopping at Sears & Roebuck than his brother's Orvis company while pulling on his left boot. His comparative analysis came to an abrupt halt when he had difficulty in putting his right foot into the second left boot.

"Needless to say, I am extremely embarrassed that Orvis could make the same mistake. Enclosed, please find a $20 gift certificate in apology for our outrageous service."

Sometimes the complaints and the correspondence were so delightful that we had to share them with the readers of the *News*. That happened in 1977, after we'd put something in the catalog that we thought of as a neat gimmick. You know the old saying about the better mousetrap. Well, we told our customers that we had found one. It was a device that was shaped like a shoebox and it caught mice alive; several of them (we said fifteen in the catalog) at a single setting. So you didn't have to reset the trap, and, if you were squeamish, you could simply move the mice somewhere without killing them. It wasn't a huge seller—disproving that old saw, anyway—but we kept it in the catalog for a couple of years.

One day, we got a letter:

Gentlemen,

I am returning under separate cover the automatic mouse-trap. We have placed this out for use and do have innumerable mice in our ranch house. However, we have caught none with this. I have had to return to the old method, as they are a pest.

The trap is in excellent condition, and I would therefore appreciate your refunding me the money. The idea seemed good, but we just never had any success with it.

I look forward to continued business with you in the future.

Sincerely,
Karen Adams

We wrote back:

Dear Mrs. Adams,

Regarding your letter . . . we are refunding your purchase price as you requested. However, inasmuch as there was a rather dead mouse in the mousetrap when it was received . . . and in view of the fact that the lady who opened the trap was less than enchanted with having to remove a rather ripe mouse, we do not feel that the trap was in any way defective.

Mrs. Adams then wrote back:

Thank you for the prompt attention to my letter. . . . Enclosed are the following:

1. a package of scented bath beads and

2. your refund check . . . in the amount of $7.50

Please give Item No. 1 to the "less than enchanted"
lady that opened our returned trap along with our apolo-
gies for such a blooper in hopes that she may receive a
small amount of pleasure from a better fragrance.

And, with Item No. 2, please apply toward the return
of [the mousetrap] to us so that we may once again put it to
apparent successful use . . .

Our best to you and all others affected at the Orvis
company for the holidays and future.

We sent the mousetrap to Mrs. Adams, along with some advice for successful operation. And I sent a separate letter, asking
her permission to quote from our correspondence in the *News*.
She replied:

Dear Mr. Perkins:

You certainly have my permission to print excerpts of my
previous correspondence . . . concerning the automatic
mousetrap.

In addition, you might note that I have since purchased 3 more of the very fine contraptions, 2 of which I
gave to others that have the same nuisance problem. We
are all finding them very effective and useful. In fact, we
have just about proven the 15-at-once theory, they are so
abundant here at the ranch.

Do you have a buffalo trap? We raise the critters here,
and this morning I had the misfortune to look out and find
about a half dozen of them in the yard . . .

Sincerely,

Some people, of course, were too impatient to write. They just
picked up the phone and called. There was a man I knew from Ohio
who called once when he'd had a little too much to drink and was

feeling exuberant. He got somebody in the order department and explained that he was about to leave on a fishing trip and there were several things that he needed before he left. The person in the order department very patiently went through everything with the caller, and they put together a fairly long list. Then, at the end of the call, my friend said, "And ask Perkins to put in anything else he thinks I might need."

Well, when I heard this, I had an idea. The year before, we'd had a concrete frog in the catalog that weighed about thirty pounds. It wasn't good for anything, just an *object* to put next to the fireplace. We sold a lot of them, so we figured the next year we'd go with concrete turtles. They didn't sell at all.

So I told the people who were packing my friend's order to put two of those turtles in with everything else. They did. And sent it out.

I never heard a word about it. I guess my friend must have just assumed he had ordered two concrete turtles along with his flies and his leaders. I can still see my friend opening his package from Orvis, scratching his head, and thinking that there must have been some reason that he thought a thirty-pound concrete turtle might turn out to be handy on a fishing trip. But *two*?

Some people called because they decided they liked talking to somebody particular in the order department. They would call again and again. And then there were the people who weren't calling to talk to anyone special but who liked to shop over the phone. They'd get somebody from the order department, and then, together, they would go through the catalog, page by page, talking about each item and deciding whether or not to order it or what color was right or how many. These people seemed inevitably to come from Texas, for some reason. They plainly had time on their hands and money to spend, and they gave us some very good orders.

Of course, not everyone was calling to talk or to browse the catalog. Some of them wanted to cuss and complain.

As I said earlier, when I bought the business, the attitude at Orvis was "the customer is usually—if not always—wrong." It took some time to change that attitude, but by the time we were taking most of our orders over the phone, everyone in the company understood, especially the people who worked the phones. Most of our people were particularly good at turning away the wrath of an angry customer with a soft voice, saying, "Yes. You're absolutely right, and we're wrong. What can we do to fix this problem?"

It almost always worked. One reason was that we gave our telephone staff total authority to solve the customer's problem, and if we had caused some aggravation through a mistake, they had the authority to send a gift certificate as well as a refund or exchange. This not only made our customers happy, it made our staff realize they were a very important part of Orvis. By the time our telephone people had worked out an exchange or whatever was necessary, a formerly angry customer would often be putting in a new order and talking about what a pleasure it was to do business with Orvis.

Of all the products Orvis has ever handled, the one that generated the most complaints by far has been waders. This was because sometime in the late sixties or early seventies, OHSA—the Occupational Health and Safety Administration—ruled that certain kinds of glues could not be used to seal the seams in rubber waders because they were dangerous to the people who manufactured the product. The companies that made waders tried all kinds of substitutes, but none of them worked very well and a lot of them didn't work at all.

Being a complete outfitter for fly fishermen, Orvis had to carry waders, and the waders had our name on them, even though we didn't make them. That didn't make any difference to the unhappy angler whose waders leaked. And he didn't care that OHSA had made it impossible to make dry waders in the United States. He wanted to complain to somebody, and the people who had sold him the waders looked like the place to start.

It got so bad that we had a system for handling the complaints. We classified complaints as Wet Ass #1, Wet Ass #2, and Wet Ass #3. The Wet Ass #1 complaint came from someone who had gone to Iceland to fish for salmon with a pair of brand-new Orvis waders that he'd never worn. When he got in the river, they leaked. When he got back, he sent in the waders with a *very* strong letter asking what we planned to do about it.

What we did was send him replacement waders, a large gift certificate, and a *very* contrite letter from me. Some people in the company thought we should include an explanation of how we didn't make the waders and that the company that did make them wasn't really at fault, either, because of the OHSA regulations. But I vetoed that. The product had the Orvis name on it, so Orvis was responsible for its suppliers' manufacturing problems, even when they were caused by OHSA. And, anyway, when you've got a wet ass, the last thing you want to hear is excuses. That's just going to make you madder.

Wet Ass #2 and #3 were complaints from people who had owned their waders longer or were fishing closer to home or for some reason didn't have reason to be quite as angry as the fellow who'd spent a week in Iceland wearing brand-new waders that leaked.

The wader problem was so serious that we had clerks in the store who would take a bathroom break anytime they saw somebody coming in the store carrying a pair of waders or even a box that looked like it might hold a pair of waders. I'd be on a fishing trip, and people would hear who I was, and they'd come over and without even introducing themselves start complaining. I started carrying an extra-large patching kit with me whenever I went someplace to fish, and I'd apologize to my disgruntled customer for the inconvenience of the leaky waders and offer to patch them. There are some pictures around the office somewhere of me bent over at the waist, with my head inside of a pair of waders, looking for the places where you could see the sunlight coming through so I could go to work with my patching kit.

It wasn't what I had in mind when I went off somewhere for a little fishing, but the customer is always right. And since I was the boss, I couldn't go hide in the bathroom.

We believed so strongly in making things good when a customer complained that we put a twenty-five-year guarantee on our graphite rods. We told the customer, "If if breaks—even if you break it—bring it back, and we'll replace it." I got some advice from people in the company who thought that we ought to put in some qualifiers about obvious abuse or intentional breakage, but I said, "We are not going to base our policies on the 1 percent of the people who are dishonest." If we were going to offer a guarantee, I didn't want to clutter it up with a lot of exceptions and fine-print qualifiers— "If it breaks, for whatever reason, Orvis will repair it as new or replace it."

We've had rods sent back for some pretty wonderful reasons. There is the all-time most common reason, which is slamming a door—especially a car door—on the tip. We've had people send the rod in asking if we'll *really* replace it after it was broken in such a bonehead manner. We tell them yes, and I think if they weren't loyal Orvis customers before, they are after that.

We've had people send in rods that were chewed up by dogs. Left on top of the car. Run over by a car. Stepped on by a horse. You can't imagine the number of ways people can find to break a fly rod. One guy sent us the rods his irate wife had broken, and another sent in one he had used to kill a rattlesnake. Someone even sent in the ashes of a rod that had been burned up in a house fire. But my own, personal, all-time favorite was from the guy whose rod had been mangled by a grizzly bear. He just wanted us to know the story—I guess he considered the mangled rod to be some kind of trophy of his survival—and he was delighted when we gave him a new rod.

The graphite rod was one of the breakthrough products during my time at Orvis, and it became a sort of company signature. But there was something inevitable about it. The graphite rod was a natu-

Leigh with his mother Katherine and two 11-foot alligators she has shot,
circa 1930.

Leigh at age three, fishing the Ochlockonee River in Georgia.

Weighing in a trophy tarpon at the Gold Cup tournament in Islamorada, Florida, in the early 1970s.

Leigh's son David with a nice brook trout in Labrador, circa 1970.

Leigh caught this small golden mahseer in the Ramaganga River, in India's Corbett National Park in 1985.

An uncommon catch—a saltwater crocodile—at Boca Paila in the Yucatan, in the early 1970s.

With wife Romi in Argentina, 1971.

With a nice permit—a saltwater fly fisherman's most sought after prize—off the Marquesas, late 1980s.

Leigh poaching "Romi's Riffle" on a Wyoming spring creek, with predictable consequences, in 1990.

Leigh with George Bush in the White House Rose Garden, at a ceremony to honor the President's Environmental Advisory Council. Leigh was a member of the Environmental Council, but in this case he appears to be advising the president on fly-casting techniques.

In the Montana hills with his English setter Midge, who has just retrieved a Hungarian partridge, mid-1990s.

RECORD CATCH CLUB
ORVIS NEWS
JULY 16, 1994   MANCHESTER, VERMONT

ANCIENT HISTORY

*Best wishes for a
happy and healthy retirement, Leigh.*

Dick Whitney

Although Leigh and I were in Williams College at the same time, we really didn't get to know each other until Leigh moved back to Cleveland. It does seem surprising that we didn't get better acquainted at Williams because we both spent most of our time at the library. Today, I doubt if either one of us could find the old library; however, I'm sure we could find Cabe's Pool Hall.

After graduation, Leigh joined Hanna on the Mesabi iron ore property—a great place for Leigh to hunt and fish, but not a place to raise a family. After a short business venture in Toledo with brother Stubb, Leigh returned to Cleveland.

With the help of National City Bank (using "Big and Friendly" as its motto) he has to tell you something), Leigh found the Harris Calorific Company. "Big and Friendly" said he needed an older and wiser leader to join him in this business, so Leigh brought in Tony Taylor, an old war horse in the Cleveland business community, to be President. Leigh went to work as Vice President in charge of sales. He covered not only the U. S. but was one of the first American businessmen to really go after global markets. While Leigh built up sales, Tony built up his son, Steve, to take over the business. Every time Leigh returned to Cleveland with a briefcase full of orders he found that Steve had been promoted in his absence.

Leigh and I were now spending more time together fishing, hunting, etc. —and for a while I was his chauffeur. The chauffeur stint was during the time that Leigh was confined to a body cast that protected his neck which he had broken when he dove into the shallow end of the Hangar pool intending to come up under a young girl to surprise her.

As a result of our conversations during the drives to and from work, Leigh and I decided to get Jim Reid's and my lawyer, John Drinko, involved in a battle to wrest control from the Taylor family. During lunch at the Union Club, John informed Leigh, Jim and me that "you don't win a pissing contest with a skunk," and "we are going to sell Leigh (at a good price) and look for a new business for him." John didn't feel that a group of young businessmen in the Cleveland community would win much favor by attacking an old business leader. In any event, this set the stage for the future. Leigh began negotiations with Tony Taylor which did not go smoothly, but eventually John accomplished his objectives—he got Leigh out and got sufficient funds to look for a new business opportunity.

Leigh took a little time off, and he and the family went on a grand safari to East Africa, where he made contacts that many of us followed; that era has passed. On his return, Leigh began a serious search for a business. We looked at steel warehousing, machine tool manufacturing, plastic fishing worms and Enterprise Manufacturing (Pflueger reels and fishing tackle). About this time, Leigh received a call from Dick Finlay, a Williams graduate, whose brother Pete had been in the AD House at Williams with Leigh. Dick told Leigh that Ducky Corkran, the owner of Orvis, might consider selling out. This sounded like a dream business for a person who loved the outdoors, hunting and fishing.

Dick Whitney and Perk Perkins, (a few years ago) each with their 15-pound plus salmon taken on a trip to Iceland.

Leigh visited Ducky and came back to Cleveland with enthusiasm and the financial figures on Orvis. John, Leigh, Jim and I—and a few others—worked the figures back and forth. We came up with the maximum purchase price that the business could go for and sent John and Leigh off to conclude the deal.

When John and Leigh sat down with Ducky at the old Orvis headquarters on Union Street, Ducky said he had no interest in selling the business unless he got $100,000 over our maximum offer (which in those days was a substantial premium). As John sized up the situation (correctly, it turned out), Ducky didn't want to sell and was just testing the market. Leigh and Ducky kept waiting for negotiations to start, and John kept making the idle chitchat. John finally said, "When are we going to have lunch—I'm getting thirsty and hungry." Ducky and Leigh looked at John in surprise. John turned to Ducky and said, "You named your price; we bought the business. Let's go have a martini and lunch." On the way out Leigh hugged at John's sleeve and said that this was considerably more than he had planned to pay. John replied, "That old son-of-a-bitch didn't want to sell the business yet, we called his bluff, and we own Orvis!"

The rest is history!

The cover of a parody issue of the *Orvis News* published on the occasion of Leigh's retirement in 1994. Inside features included an exposé about how Leigh paid for an Orvis fly rod with a bad check while a college student and photographs of him being dumped unceremoniously from the back of a mule. (Courtesy of The Orvis Company, Inc.)

Leigh ties a fly to a tippit.

Leigh with sons Perk and Dave (with beard) after receiving a Chevron Conservation Award in 1994. (Courtesy of The Orvis Company, Inc.)

With a twenty-five-inch brown trout taken from Montana's Blackfoot River.

Dave and his daughter, Hannah, with a rainbow trout taken from the pond at Leigh's home in Manchester, Vermont, 1992.

With his grandson Simon and two fine bonefish in the Bahamas, mid-1990s.

ral step, even though there were a lot of possible pitfalls along the
way.

But there were other products that came to be just as tightly
tied up with the Orvis image that came to us almost spontaneously.
These are products that people—especially our customers—asso-
ciate intimately with Orvis but that came to us out of the blue.

In 1970, I was visiting a gift show in Chicago, and, among
all the various products on display, I noticed that someone had
bundled up a few splinters of wood and called it starter kindling.
I was reminded of what we used to call in Georgia "fatwood," back
when I was a boy. It came from old long-leaf pine stumps, and we
used it for kindling. My parents' guests from the North would always want to take a box of it home with them.

Fatwood was a regional colloquialism, used in a small area
of south Georgia and north Florida. In other areas, the same stuff
was called by many other names, including "lighterwood" and "fat
lighter" and "heart pine." But whatever it is called, it sure as hell
works. The wood is saturated in pine resin so that you can light it
with just the touch of a match. It beats kerosene or coal oil for starting a fire, and it is a lot more pleasing in the fireplace.

Fatwood comes mostly from the stumps of trees cut a hundred years ago, since it forms only in the heart of overmature long-
leaf pine, and with today's forestry practices, very few trees last
that long. When the virgin forests were cleared, the trees were cut
down by crews using cross-cut handsaws that worked just about
waist high. This left a tall stump, and the heart pine never rotted.
Local people had gathered a little for their own use, but most of
those fatwood stumps were still standing, full of resin and ready
to be cut, packaged, and marketed a century later.

So I talked to Norwood Willis, the superintendent of May's
Pond, the place down in Florida that my father had left to me.
Norwood was a north Florida native and a very resourceful man
who didn't need a lot of supervision. He understood right away
what I wanted, and he went to work. He found some old pulp and
timber cutters who knew the woods and would go back into the

forest and salvage the old fatwood stumps as long as it turned a dollar.

After they brought it in, Norwood's crew sawed it up and split it into splinters and packaged it into neat bundles with a handle. We put fatwood in the catalog and in the store, and it sold like wildfire, no pun intended. I had figured that only a few people would know about fatwood, that it would be a regional thing. But I was wrong. People from Connecticut to California wanted it. That first year, it was a huge success and the runaway best-seller of all our hard goods. Today, it is still one of our best-selling products, and it is getting so we have to look farther and farther to find the old long-leaf stumps.

Fatwood had one unqualified advantage as a product. The consumer buys it to burn it up, so he's always going to need more.

We came up with another of those signature products in 1977, when Orvis was just passing the $10 million mark in annual sales and things were looking good. It was another one of those products that couldn't have been simpler and that the consumer, once he saw it, knew he had to have.

We had a visitor in Vermont who noted that we had a lot of dogs around the house. Two pointing dogs and one Lab, at least, and sometimes more. I've *always* had dogs, and they've always stayed inside and usually slept in my bedroom. So our visitor, who was from Wales, sent us three of what were called Dog Nests over there. They were really nothing more than bean bags suitable for a dog to get comfortable on, and they were sold in a few pet stores in England almost as a novelty. But when I saw how my dogs took to them, I knew that this was a product we could move.

We negotiated with the woman in England who had come up with the name Dog Nest and we copyrighted it for use in the United States. Then we put them in the catalog, where they were an instant hit. People loved them, and I know their dogs loved them even more. They were just the thing for people who wanted to pamper their dogs and make them comfortable, and they also appealed to people who didn't love their dogs so much as they wanted to keep them off the furniture. The Dog Nest became such a successful product that it made more sense for us to make them ourselves—they were so bulky—and reduce costs than to contract the work out to a vendor. So we began producing the polystyrene beads ourselves and filling the nests on a daily basis. Today, many of our competitors carry a similar product without the name Dog Nest, but we still sell over $1.3 million worth annually.

We've had two recurring, minor complaints about Dog Nests, which is a pretty small number compared to all the satisfied customers and happy dogs. One complaint goes something like, "My dog doesn't like the nest because it makes a noise when he gets on it." My answer to that one is, "Mister, if I had a dog like that, I wouldn't tell anyone." I don't say that, of course, and Orvis cheerfully sends refunds to the owners of those wimpy dogs.

The other complaint is that a certain type of dog, with a kind of defiant temperament, will chew up the nest, especially when he is ticked off at his master. I had one such dog, and when she went after that nest, it made a hell of a mess. The tiny beads would go everywhere, and since they are electrostatic, they stick to everything. One irate customer wrote me a strong letter saying that his Fido's Dog Nest had practically caused him a divorce. He had to clean the mess up, and when he was finished, he had four plastic garbage bags full of dog-nest innards that he was personally going to come and dump in my office.

I rather looked forward to that encounter, but he never showed up.

Chapter 10

The Dogs of Sport

I might not have recognized the potential of Dog Nests if I hadn't felt the way I do about dogs. It goes back to the old principle in business—especially retail—of knowing your market and knowing your customer. The same way it took a fly fisherman to recognize the potential of the Zinger, the way I did when I saw it on the waitress's chest, it took a dog person to recognize the appeal of the Dog Nest. And I have always been a dog person.

In fact, dogs make up a big piece of the sporting life for me. The kinds of hunting that I enjoy just about inevitably involve dogs. I've gone on driven shoots in England, Scotland, and all over the world, and while I certainly enjoy that kind of shooting—and that is a distinction the English insist on: when you are "hunting," you are with a dog, and when you are "shooting," you are not—I much prefer being in the field with a dog. You might shoot at a hundred birds on a good driven shoot, while you can work all day for a dozen shots hunting quail and one or two hunting grouse in a bad year, but if you are like me, the size of the bag and the amount of shooting is nowhere near as important to the enjoyment of the game as the dog work. It is the payoff. There are sportsmen who like to sit around the fire at night and talk about guns, and there are those who like to talk about dogs. Put me in the second group.

I've had a lot of dogs in my life. Many of them memorable, and for different reasons.

The first of those memorable dogs was a pit bull. A cousin of mine gave me the dog when it was a pup and I was eight or nine. My cousin was older and had a little mischief in her, and I think she believed—rightly—that a pit bull pup would enhance my propensity for getting in trouble.

I named the dog Tippy, and he was the first really important thing in my life. He was a loving, constant companion made of solid muscle with considerable speed. But, unfortunately, true to his breed, he was a killing machine. That was the bad news. The good news was that my father despised cats, and Tippy killed every cat that showed up at our farm. I can remember a number of times watching, horrified, as a cat would bow his back and bare his teeth as Tippy sped toward him. One shake of Tippy's head, and the cat would go in the air about ten feet and land lifeless.

Tippy got along well with most dogs, but when one challenged him, that was the end of that dog. The worst scene I remember happened in the yard of our neighbors, who were very fancy New York people. They rented my grandfather's house next door to our house for the summer and one day had a big Sunday tea party on the front porch. When Tippy wandered over to check out the party, their springer spaniel challenged him. It was the right thing to do, since it was the springer's territory, but he picked the wrong dog. Tippy chased the spaniel under the front porch where the party was going on and proceeded to kill him. My father gently explained that we were going to have to find another home for Tippy, and I was smart enough to suspect that it would be a grave. I can't remember how it happened, and I'm sure there were a lot of tears involved, but I somehow won Tippy's pardon.

After this performance, Tippy developed the unacceptable habit of pulling paper boys off their bicycles. He didn't ever bite them; he just wanted to dismount them. This, however, wasn't much comfort to the paper boys, who were scared half to death. The parents of one of these boys finally called the sheriff.

This was really big trouble, and I knew I couldn't talk Tippy out of this one, so I ran away with him and hid in the woods overnight. Once again, my salesmanship prevailed, and I won another pardon for Tippy, who, somehow or other, survived to live a long and destructive life.

Tippy was not a proper sporting dog, of course, and neither was my next memorable dog. The story of Black Mac begins in Ontario, where I'd gone with my mother and father on a fishing trip when I was twelve. There was a dog in camp that was just about the smartest dog I had ever seen. The camp owner called her a black-and-tan rat terrier, and she could find a ball no matter where I had hidden it, even if it was ten feet up in a tree or two hundred yards away with the dog locked in the house so she couldn't watch me hide it.

I had a wonderful time with that dog, and the camp owner kindly informed me that she was about to have puppies. He said that if I wanted one, he'd send it to me. God knows who the father was, but I like to think it was a Lab because, when my pup arrived, he looked like a miniature Lab with a big white splotch on his chest.

Black Mac was an important part of my life for a long time. He was smart as hell and arrogant for a mongrel. His two great talents were dove retrieving and rat catching. He was the best dove marker I've ever seen, and when the two of us were together on a dove field, I'd always know when there were birds coming in by the way he'd stiffen up and get ready. He'd see them a long time before I would, and if I was looking the wrong way, he'd whine until I looked in the right direction. He was more eyes than nose, but he rarely missed a downed dove no matter how far it flew on before it fell. If I wasn't shooting well, he'd start whining, and if I kept on missing, he'd howl, and then, finally, he'd just leave me and move over to somebody else who could hit birds so he could pick them up. That kind of irritated me.

But his real specialty was ratting. We'd go down to the horse barn after dark, and I'd turn the lights on and swing the upper half of the stall doors open. Rats would often be behind these, and I would sweep them off their perches with a broom. I'd put as many as three rats on the ground at one time, and Mac would nail them all before they could get to cover. One time, I put him in a partially empty corn crib that was just loaded with rats. As I remember, he killed eighteen in less than a minute and a half. It was a sight to behold, and Mac knew he was hot stuff.

He also loved to go fishing with me. One evening, we came home late from a fishing trip, and I had kept a couple of big bass alive because I wanted to stock them in another pond. So I put them in the bathtub in my room at Spring Hill, our Georgia home, and Mac checked on them about every half hour. Every year after that, when we'd first take Mac back to Georgia, usually at Thanksgiving time, he couldn't wait to run in and look in that bathtub to see if any bass were there. This went on for five years.

As I mentioned, Mac was an arrogant little dog, and he thought he could whip the world. He picked a lot of fights, and he lost most of them. But that didn't stop him. Not until he took on a six-foot rattlesnake. No one was around to see the fight, but we found them both dead, not very far apart.

I got my first bird dog when I was a sophomore at Williams. I'd been around plenty of bird dogs—especially in Georgia, hunting quail with English pointers and setters—but I'd never had one that was mine and lived with me. Those dogs in Georgia lived in a kennel at the place and were trained by a dog handler who reported to my mother. Actually, that first bird dog of mine was supposed to have been her dog.

In 1946, somebody gave my mother a Brittany spaniel, which was a brand-new dog in the United States. There were only a few of them around. They'd been brought back from France, I suppose, by soldiers coming home from the war, and they were nowhere near as popular as they are today. Most people had never heard of them.

But my mother was very pleased with this Brittany and wanted to breed him. She'd heard about a Brittany bitch in Keene, New Hampshire, which wasn't that far from Williams, and she wanted me to go check the dog out.

I drove over, and the owner took me hunting with the dog, whose name was Leda, and who put on a hell of show, pointing and holding both woodcock and grouse, which I believe is one of the real tests of a dog. Grouse are wary and unpredictable. They will move on a dog, and if she gets too close, they will flush. They will also flush wild and just generally make life hard for even a well-trained dog with a good nose. But Leda could handle them. I fell in love with that dog on the spot and gave the owner all the money I had in my pocket for a down payment and said I would send the rest by check. Leda went back to Williams with me.

She became my roommate, which was okay at Williams, where dogs were something of a tradition. There were all kinds of strays that were adopted by the various fraternities. Leda was a class act compared to most of them, and we spent every weekend of bird season out hunting.

Some time later, I was on the phone with my mother, and she mentioned that she had asked me to check on a dog and I had failed to follow through. She was in Georgia at the time.

"No, Mother," I said. "I did exactly what you asked me to do. It turned out to be a wonderful dog, and I bought it."

"Well," she said, "when are you sending it down?"

"I'm not," I said. "I'm keeping her with me. She's my roommate."

Well, in truth, I did keep Leda, but she also went to Georgia with me on Christmas vacations, and she generally stayed down there after I went back to school since the hunting season was already over in New England and had a couple of months to run down south. Leda did well in Georgia and even became a star for doing something no other dog down there had ever done.

We had wild turkeys in the woods back then, and one of the ways we hunted them in the fall was to drive them off their roost just before dawn, over a line of six to eight guns. The turkeys would fly over at tree-top level, about thirty yards up, and the only way to kill them was to hit them in the head. This meant that there were some birds knocked down with broken wings, and they would run off and usually couldn't be recovered, since a turkey—even a wounded one—can run faster than a horse in the woods.

My parents were putting on one of these turkey drives one morning, and one of their guests was an army general—I don't remember his name—who knocked a turkey down but didn't kill it. He insisted on putting on a search for that turkey, and his attitude was that he was the general and his desires would be treated like orders. Well, my mother wanted to get everyone out of the woods and back to the house for breakfast, so she told the general that she would get somebody to bring a dog in and look for the turkey. She had no idea at all that it would work—it never had, but she needed to do something, and it seemed to mollify the general.

So one of the hands, a man named Buddy, went back to the kennel and brought Leda out and put her in the woods, sniffing around where the general's turkey had gone down. Leda had never met a turkey, but she picked up the scent and took off cold-trailing that wounded turkey. Some time later, Buddy heard Leda barking, and after a while, he found her. She had trailed that turkey for half a mile and killed it, but the turkey was too big for her to retrieve. Everyone was thoroughly surprised, but it was no freak. She did it again on other hunts, and after a while, she got to be famous around the other plantations. People would call up and invite Mother or Father to go on their turkey drives, so Leda could come along and cold-trail those wounded birds. She once trailed and killed a bird two miles from where it was downed.

She was just a sensational dog, smart and very determined, and when she went with me to Minnesota, where I hunted grouse and woodcock, she showed some real versatility by helping me round up an escaped pig that belonged to a family that lived next to a mine where I was the foreman.

They came to me for help, and I said I would see what I could do after the shift. I didn't have much experience capturing fugitive pigs and didn't really know how I was going to go about it. So I went home and got Leda, and after a while, we spotted the pig lying on the ground near a pile of burning aspen. Leda had pointed and retrieved just about every kind of game bird, but she did not chase deer or rabbits. I didn't expect her to herd pigs, either, but when this one got up to run, I yelled, "Sic 'em, Leda." That isn't a term you generally use with bird dogs, but Leda took off after that pig, caught up with it, grabbed it by the ear, and rolled it over on the ground. Now the pig weighed more than eighty pounds, and Leda was barely thirty-five. Needless to say, the pig had no trouble shaking Leda off. But she went back after that pig. They'd roll around, and the pig would take off, and Leda would go back after it. Finally, I caught up with them. The pig was squealing its head off on top of Leda, and I thought the pig was killing my dog. But not at all—Leda had him by the ear, and the pig was squealing for mercy.

I don't remember anyone being as grateful as those old pensioners, living in a railroad car at the edge of the mine, when I dragged that pig home.

Leda was with me all the way through Minnesota and the mines, until I went back to Cleveland, where I hunted with her and one of her pups. And then I had a granddaughter of Leda's named Dessie, who was a hell of a good dog. Maybe the best pointing dog I've ever owned. Very intense. But that dog was killed on the highway, not long after I took over Orvis and moved to Vermont. Then there was Pepper, who was the end of the line that had started with Leda.

Next came a half setter and half Brittany named Tubby, before I got into pure setters with another memorable dog whose name was Douglas.

That dog came to me in a sort of interesting way. When I was serving as president of the Ruffed Grouse Society, which is a conservation organization, there was a man named Sam Kirkwood who was head of the biochemistry department at the University of Minnesota and trained setters as a hobby. He got in touch and said he would make me the same offer he had made the last three presidents of the society. He would select a puppy for the serving president of the society to buy. Sam would keep the puppy and train it, and at seven months it would be fully trained. If the president decided that he didn't want the dog, then Sam would buy it back.

Well, I'd grown up around some pretty good dog trainers, and most of them didn't even start working with a bird dog until it was a year old and didn't expect it to be close to finished for a year after that. So I was curious and took this fellow up on his offer. When it came time, I went out to Minnesota to look at this pup, and sure enough, even though it wasn't even fully grown, it was absolutely steady on birds. The only thing was, the dog had an unorthodox way of pointing birds—he'd sit down. It wasn't exactly the calendar-art pose you expect from a bird dog, but it worked. Douglas was a very effective dog in the field and a funny old guy. When he sat down and looked down his nose at the ground, you could be 100 percent sure it was a bird and that it was right there. If he was standing up, it could be a rabbit, a box turtle, or a snake. In fact, down in Florida once, Douglas went on a rigid point right near the house. He was pointing an eight-foot alligator and wasn't taking any chances on sitting down. I got Douglas in 1980, and I've had setters around ever since. I still hunt with his daughter Midge and his grandson Reb.

My dog universe really expanded about five years before I got Douglas. I had continued going down to the family place, Spring Hill, in Georgia for vacations and Christmas until the early seventies, when I built my own house at Mays Pond, the plantation that my father had left me when he died. At first, I shared dogs and expenses with my mother, who kept a kennel at Mays Pond. But sometime around 1975, I began to develop my own string. I still had a Brittany or two, but I felt I needed some big running dogs, and the traditional breed was the English pointer. And some people used setters. So I told my manager, Norwood Willis, to start looking for some bird dogs. His first acquisition was Sam.

Back then, some of the local boys would hunt dogs for a season and then turn them loose so they wouldn't have to feed them through the summer. Come fall, they would beg, borrow, or steal a dog for the new hunting season. The local sheriff had picked up a couple of these unfortunate strays, and one of them was in such bad shape that he had to be put down. He called Norwood and told him that the other young dog looked pretty good and did Norwood want to take a look. Well, he did, and that dog turned out to be Sam, a liver-and-white pointer, and another one of my memorable bird dogs.

After considerable attention from the vet to get him over the heartworm and other worms and skin infections he had picked up, Sam was ready for some training and then the field, where he turned out to be an outstanding performer, one of the best. Sam just knew how to find birds. Even if the scenting conditions were lousy—hot, dry, the middle of the day—you'd put Sam down and he'd find birds. He just seemed to know, somehow, where they'd be. He'd find them, and he'd point them.

But Sam had one bad habit. After he'd found the birds and pointed them, and we'd gotten down from the mule wagon or off horseback and shot them, he liked to eat them. Maybe he'd developed a taste for them when he was running wild, I don't know. But whenever you knocked down a bird that Sam had pointed, it would be a mad race to see who could get to it first. If Sam won, the bird would end up in the quail hash department.

Sam was the only English pointer I ever brought up to Vermont to make a grouse dog—and a house dog—out of. I kept a lot of pointers in my kennel down south, sometimes as many as twenty, but they were all working dogs that I never got to know personally the way I did my Brittanys, my setters, and Sam.

He was no problem at all to break as a house dog, and he handled grouse like a champ. But you had to run like hell to beat him to a downed bird because he liked the flavor of grouse even better than he liked quail. He ended up with a couple of knots on his head, from my 20-gauge barrels, but he never did learn to stop eating birds. I'm sure many English pointers would make fine house dogs. Like most of his breed, Sam lived to hunt. When he was in the house, he was quiet, pleasant, and unobtrusive. He now rests in the dog graveyard, with my other favorite dogs, near my home in Vermont.

Of all the pointing dogs I've owned, the one I've probably spent the most time with is Midge, who was just coming into her peak years when I retired. So Midge and I have spent as many as 150 days hunting in a year. You get to know each other pretty well when you spend that much time together.

In September, we hunted Montana for Hungarian partridge and sharptails and sage grouse. Then we went to New England in October for ruffed grouse and woodcock and back to Montana for pheasant and on to Florida for quail and, finally, to New Mexico for desert quail. It was a real sportsman's odyssey, and Midge was a good companion and a great performer in the field.

I've had a good many bird dogs that would learn to circle birds and pin them down, but none who could do it with the finesse Midge showed. On woodcock, a bird that will hold tight, Midge would make a very small circle, not more than ten feet in diameter, pointing from three different angles so you knew exactly where the bird was. On grouse, which will run on the ground and can flush if you crowd them, she would circle wider—say, fifteen yards. On quail, the circle might be twenty-five yards, and on pheasant, as much as seventy-five. Invariably, she would hold the birds and tell you, by the way she was pointing, exactly where they were.

On one occasion, when I was hunting sharptail on a very high hill in Montana and the cover was extremely sparse, just a few stunted pines on the hillside, my partner said, "You know, your dog is running in circles around those three little pine trees over there."

We made our way in that direction, and as we got closer, we could see the sharptails' heads in among the trees. Midge had figured out that if she pointed them, they were going to run out in the opposite direction where there was no grass cover at all and they would just flush. So she herded them just like a sheep dog, keeping them right where they were until we could get in range. My friend came up with a pretty slick alibi after we both missed easy shots. He said he was dizzy from watching Midge run around in circles.

Midge had another interesting quirk. I took her duck hunting one day when we were short of Labs. Normally, setters aren't considered retrieving dogs, but she did an incredible job. She had always liked water, and, with no training at all, she sat quietly in the duck blind until the time came to retrieve, and then she brought in every one of my ducks like an old pro. She really enjoyed herself.

Later that season, while hunting quail on horseback, I put Midge out to work, and she simply refused to move. She gave me this strange look, as if to say, "I'm not hunting with you today." She didn't. Not that day or the next day, either. It was a week before she agreed to hunt with me again on horseback. If I was walk-shooting, she would go with me, so apparently she had decided she was having a midlife career change, and from now on, quail hunting on horseback was out. I guess she figured that if she was going to run at her age, then I could damn well get down off my horse and walk with her. A year before, she had been top quail dog out of sixteen good dogs. She still enjoyed her duck hunting, grouse, and woodcock, or any other kind of game as long as I was afoot. But no more hunting off horse or wagon for Midge.

Sometimes I think dogs are more like people than people are. This is especially true when it comes to Labs.

I got my first retriever when I was working in the mines and taking advantage of the good duck hunting opportunities around Minnesota. Ever since then, I've owned at least one Lab, usually more, and couldn't imagine being without one. No breed has more personality.

One of the most memorable of the many Labs I've owned was a dog named Hannah. My wife, Romi, acquired the dog, which annoyed me a little since I thought I was the big expert on dogs, and what did she know about choosing a Labrador? Of course, Hannah turned out to be one of the most delightful, satisfactory dogs we've ever had.

Hannah was a character even when she was a pup. The first spring we had her, in 1974, my daughter, Molly, was with us in Vermont. Molly was always a terrific animal person, and she noticed that the mallard duck that had been nesting on the pond in front of our farmhouse had left one duckling behind, still pecking its way out of the shell. Molly brought the duckling inside and caught bugs for it and nursed it along until it got on its short little legs. She intended to return the duck to its family, but it had totally imprinted on Molly and waddled along behind her wherever she went. Molly even tried diving into the pond, so that the little duck would follow her close to its mother and brothers and sisters and join the brood. But no dice; the duckling stuck with Molly.

Hannah, who was only eight weeks old, met the duck when it was eight days old. Hannah had all the proper instincts and knew, deep down, that she was supposed to be a duck dog. So she and the duckling would play cowboys and Indians, but Hannah never harmed the duck. And when the games were over and it was nap time, they would cuddle up together and go to sleep. It was just about the cutest thing I have ever seen in my life.

When Hannah grew up, she turned out to be an outstanding retriever. She was also just about the smartest dog I've ever known. She understood things that made you wonder how she did it. She was great at marking birds, and she would see them a long time before I did. I'd known a lot of dogs that would do that, going back to Black Mac, but Hannah could do more than that.

I remember one time when we were out in a cypress and gum pond down in Florida in the early morning hunting for wood ducks and teal. This kind of shooting only lasts for a half hour or so, and the light is so weak when it starts that the ducks will often sail in and land on the water right next to you before they get wise and explode out of the pond. Hannah and I were sitting on a little platform built onto a gum tree, and we'd had some shooting. She'd already retrieved a wood duck and three teal that morning, when another woodie sneaked in on us and landed about forty feet away, then swam immediately behind a cypress tree. It wasn't abnormal behavior for a duck to light and swim away like that, and normally Hannah wouldn't have paid any attention. She would have been looking at the sky to mark more incoming ducks.

It was light by now, and I'd gotten a clear look at that duck. To me, it looked perfectly healthy. But Hannah knew better and immediately dove into the pond and swam after it. She swam out of sight, with me yelling after her, afraid that she might run into an alligator. Usually, she was pretty obedient, but she didn't pay any attention, and I thought I might have to get down and go wading after her. After about five minutes, she came back with that duck, dead in her mouth. It had obviously been wounded by someone hunting in another part of the pond—there was shooting going on around us—but how Hannah knew is beyond me.

Hannah developed these trademark stunts. One of her most memorable ones occurred whenever we went on a duck shoot at my place in Florida. The hunting party, which might be as large as eight people, would come home with as many as twenty ducks in the back of the station wagon, and Hannah would immediately dismount and search through that pile of ducks until she found the most unusual specimen of the day. She would then take that duck into the house and show it off to all the other dogs and to any family member or guest who hadn't made it up for the shoot.

I could almost always tell which duck she was going to pick. To show off, I'd tell my guests, "Now watch this. Hannah will go to the back of the station wagon and pick out the female redhead and take it into the house." Hannah and I knew, since this was the first hen redhead we'd shot all year, that it was no contest. But my guests would be impressed. One day, I confidently said that she would pick the drake pintail we'd shot that morning, but Hannah fooled me and picked a snipe. It wasn't a duck, but it was certainly an unusual bag. So she was consistent, and I wasn't sharp enough to figure it out.

Hannah loved to show off. She had another trick. Whenever we brought out a bottle of champagne, which she recognized the instant it came out of the refrigerator, she would get all excited. When the cork was popped, she'd catch it when it came off the ceiling—usually on the fly. Then she'd present it to Romi, like it was a duck she had retrieved.

We had another pretty remarkable black Lab named Mitzi. She was unquestionably the smartest dog of any breed we've ever had and the best retriever. She took her job very seriously and was extremely good at it. After a shoot, she would circle around the edge of the pond to round up cripples that had crawled off into the woods. She often found more ducks than anyone realized had been hit, and nobody had trained her to do this. She learned it on her own.

She had another duck-pond trick. When she'd retrieve a duck to the blind, she would roll it over daintily on its back and then nose it up into line with the ducks she had already retrieved, so that they were belly up in a neat row. Finally, she would touch each duck with her nose, as though she were counting them.

There was something else she figured out all on her own, and it didn't have anything to do with ducks. My daughter, Molly, invited a boy up from New York when she was fifteen years old. The little twerp refused to stay in our guest house because he didn't want to stay in a house all alone. The only alternative was to put him in the guest bedroom right across from Molly's room. Romi was somewhat concerned about this arrangement, and in ways I never understood, managed to convey this to Mitzi. When everybody went off to bed, Mitzi, who always slept at the foot of our bed, was nowhere to be found. We looked all around the house and went outside and called but couldn't find her. Finally, Romi went upstairs and found her in the hall between Molly's room and the guest room. We called her, but she wouldn't leave, and that's where she slept for two nights, until the little twerp left and she could return to her accustomed Dog Nest.

My current Lab may be the greatest character of any dog I have ever owned. He is a big yellow Lab who was given to me as a pup by some friends from Cleveland. They had already named him

Bernie because they were fans of the Cleveland Browns, who, in those days, had a quarterback named Bernie Kosar. Anyway, the name fit.

Bernie was big and clumsy, even when he was a pup. He had a way of knocking things over when he moved through a room. The older he got, the more trouble he got in. He was at some friends' house once and somehow opened the door to their pantry and got out a country ham wrapped in cheesecloth. He ate just about the whole thing, cheesecloth included, and then drank all the water in every toilet in the house, he was so thirsty from the salty meat.

One day I was taking my ten-year-old grandson, Simon, on his first duck hunt. Bernie was with us, and we were all pretty excited. Simon was already showing signs of being a great shot. Just that week, he'd been given his first chance on wild quail and killed a bird on his first covey rise. This morning, on the duck pond, he did it again, nailing a green-winged teal as it zipped in at daylight.

Bernie, typically, was looking off in the wrong direction, and when I told him to fetch, he made a big splashy entrance and swam away from the duck. After some loud persuading, he returned to the starting point, where Simon tossed a corncob at the duck to show Bernie the right direction. The corncob landed about a foot from the duck, which was lying in open water, belly up. Bernie swam out very purposefully and nosed the duck out of the way so he could retrieve the corncob. Simon was fast losing respect for both my dog-training expertise and my dog. Finally, after a lot of clowning around and much yelling, we got Bernie sorted out and he brought in the duck.

A friend of mine came up with the theory that Bernie realizes that a lot of dogs have been reliable, consistent performers but that only special dogs become comic legends. And Bernie is in the business of creating a legend. He likes people, and he likes for people to talk about him. On a dove field, for instance, he will retrieve the first couple of birds I knock down, but then he decides it is time to go calling. So he runs all around the field, stopping to visit with all the shooters for a while, before he finally comes back to me and goes to work. On a duck pond, he pays as much attention to his diving style as he does to his retrieving. He looks like an Olympic gold medalist going into the water. When he brings a bird back to the quail wagon, he prances with his head held up high, so he looks like he is taking a victory lap. He has a lot of style, and he makes a lot of friends. He has been written up three or four times in magazine stories. Friends of mine who call just to check in and talk always ask, "How's Bernie?"

Another friend of mine once said to me, after Romi had kicked Bernie out of the house for about the millionth time, "I know why Romi gets so mad at Bernie. It's because he's so much like you."

Bernie has been a great companion and has made me laugh a lot. But I can say that about many dogs. There is much to be said for the sporting life and all of its pleasures and satisfactions. It certainly has been good for me and brought me a lot of happiness. And one of the best parts of the sporting life, by far, is that you get to hang around with a lot of interesting dogs.

Chapter 11

Further Travels in the Wide World of Sport

As my business grew, so did my contacts around the world. I had always enjoyed traveling, especially when there was some hunting or fishing in it, and now I had opportunities to go to some of the most desirable spots in the world to enjoy some of the very best sport anywhere. Often, these opportunities came in the form of invitations from people I'd never met.

One of these invitations came out of the blue, from a salesman for a Scottish fly-tying outfit we did some business with. This fellow was over in the States, calling on us, and said that I should bring one of my boys over to Scotland some time for what he called some "rough shooting." I assumed that rough shooting meant casual or informal, as opposed to the driven shoots, which can be kind of fancy-dress affairs, with everyone wearing tweeds and following a lot of elaborate rituals. I said I would take him up on his invitation, and, later that year, I did.

I was going to be in Iceland, salmon fishing, and it seemed like a good time. I'd told the salesman who had extended the invitation that I was coming and that I was bringing my son Dave.

We flew to Wick, Scotland, from Reykjavik, via London, and the salesman met us at the airport. I noticed that he seemed a bit nervous. After about an hour's drive, he delivered us to a palatial-looking manor house, which he explained was the Forsinard Estate, owned by Teddy Tyron-Wilson, the principal owner of the fly-tying company he worked for. Dave and I had in mind, when we'd been invited to do some rough shooting, that we'd stay in a pub and go out with the local boys. But now it was becoming painfully clear that this was going to be a real upscale operation. The salesman got our bags out of the car and was about to leave when I asked him if he wasn't staying. He announced that he'd never in his life been permitted to shoot at Forsinard. I was beginning to think that he might not have even announced to our host that he'd invited us to shoot there, but as he drove off, we were welcomed warmly by our host, Teddy Tyron-Wilson, who had servants take us, and our meager luggage, to our rooms. As we made our way down the vast halls and up the sweeping stairs, we passed other guests who were making their way down for evening cocktails, and then dinner, dressed in black tie and formal wear. Now we knew we were in real trouble.

Dave, who was twelve, and I had one necktie between us, and it sure as hell wasn't black. Our clothing bore the evidence of a week of salmon fishing in a very crude camp without benefit of laundry. All we had done to get ready for this visit was pack and stop at an airport shop to buy a house gift, which was a small jar of lumpfish caviar. We were way out of our league.

We cleaned up as well as we possibly could, but it wasn't anywhere near good enough. I was hoping that our host would have us eat in the kitchen. But not at all; he and his guests couldn't have been more friendly and cordial. The rest of the guests were Lord This and Lady That with a sprinkling of Brigadier So and So thrown in. The drinks and conviviality before dinner were reassuring, and I was beginning to forget what a scruffy-looking Yank I was. Then Dave came over and whispered to me, "Dad, let's not give them that gift." He pointed to a silver bowl sitting on a table and piled full of the real stuff—about half a gallon of Beluga caviar.

I agreed with Dave's suggestion and felt, more than ever, like a scruffy Yank.

But dinner was most gracious and elegant, and afterward, I had my first experience, since Minnesota and the mines, of the ladies departing and leaving the men to their talk. Only here, the men passed around a bottle of port and smoked cigars. I didn't smoke cigars at the time, but I really got into the port and was beginning to think I was one of the regulars around there. So I piped up and said something about how this was pretty good port and where could I get some.

"You can't," I was told, politely but firmly.

I found out later that this gaffe was something like asking a rancher out West how many cattle he has on his spread.

The next day, Dave and I found out what rough shooting in northern Scotland was all about. The term didn't mean there was something casual or informal about the way you did things. It was merely a way to distinguish what you were doing from a classic driven shoot where you stay in one place and beaters move the game to you.

There were eight of us, and, except for Dave and me, everyone was dressed in tweeds, plus fours, and Barbour coats. The method of hunting was to walk in a straight line about fifteen yards apart, with several Labs at heel. The hunters would flush the birds ahead of them, unexpectedly, and when one was downed, a Lab would go out and retrieve it. A couple of the lords' and brigadiers' wives came along for the exercise but did not carry guns. We got about a dozen or so red grouse in half a day, and it was lots of exercise and good sport, though nothing like shooting over a pointing dog.

That evening, our host was kind enough to ask the rest of his guests to dress down so the scruffy Yanks wouldn't feel so conspicuous. The lords and the brigadiers did their damnedest, but they couldn't dress down to our standard. Still, we were made to feel very much at home, and I appreciated the gesture. Dave was extremely popular with the group, even though it was not their custom to have young boys hunting with the seniors. I don't know what we did to deserve it, but Teddy Tyron-Wilson became a good friend as a result of that trip. He has come to our place, Mays Pond, in Florida several times for quail and duck hunting, and we've been back to his place for a number of shoots. And Romi sees to it that I'm a little better prepared in terms of my wardrobe.

Another one of those surprise invitations came when a vice president from American Airlines called and said the company had just opened a new route to New Zealand and wanted to promote it in the in-flight magazine. Would my wife and I be interested in traveling to New Zealand—first class and all expenses paid—to research and write about the wonderful fly-fishing there? I wasn't a writer by profession, but Romi is pretty good, and I didn't have any trouble at all persuading her. I was pretty eager, myself, having been exposed briefly to New Zealand fly-fishing on a short stop-over there when I was with Harris Calorific. And like everyone in the fly-fishing community, I'd heard the stories about the wonderfully clear rivers and the very large, very wary trout.

We flew to Christchurch in the South Island on American's scheduled flight. From there, we had to take a single-engine charter flight over the Remarkable Mountains to Te Anu, where the Takaro Club Lodge we would be visiting had a landing strip. The Remarkables are spectacular, but when the pilot dipped the wing so we could admire the view, Romi's remarks were not entirely appreciative. She is no fan of single-engine planes and especially not when they are weaving between mountain peaks in bad weather. To top off the experience, the pilot had trouble finding the lodge since the buildings had sod roofs and were virtually invisible from above.

But we finally arrived, and when we were on the ground, we were flabbergasted by the accommodations and the staff. It was an extraordinary place, owned and developed by a very wealthy American family. We were told that the driveway alone cost a couple of million dollars, and that was in 1972. There was a superb Austrian chef on a staff that worked out to about four people per guest. If you changed your clothes for dinner, by the time you got back to the room, your laundry was washed, pressed, folded, and placed in a drawer. They even had a Takaro Club tie—for scruffy Americans, no doubt.

Our host, whose name was Stockton Rush, couldn't have been more genial or the other guests more attractive. The only negative to the trip was the guide we were assigned on the first day.

He was certainly competent and knew his stuff, but he didn't seem interested in whether his clients enjoyed themselves or had any fun. He almost seemed to prefer that they didn't.

The first river he took us to was called the Whitestone. It had gin-clear water that you could cross at the riffles without getting your ankles wet. Between the riffles, there were pools that would often hold one or two mammoth brown trout. Our guide intoned that presentation to these fish was everything and a bad cast could put them down forever. He made it abundantly clear that he didn't think we'd have the skills to do the job. He also explained, helpfully, that our tackle was no good. One had to use a dark-colored line, or the fish would certainly spook. He provided us with reels that held dark line.

After lining me up on the first pool, he explained helpfully that it could be a mile to another pool where we'd find fish, so I'd better make my first cast count. Much to his delight, my first cast was something less than perfect and the fish spooked. We moved on to the next pool.

After a stealthy approach, I took a fish on the first cast. It was a beautiful, five-and-a-half-pound male brown that leaped magnificently, and I was delighted. The guide held the fish for a photo, released it, and explained courteously, "That fish's name is Knucklehead, and you're the fifth client to catch him. Any damn fool could catch this fish."

I suppose a little humility is good for the soul, and this guide certainly provided me with a generous portion. But not enough to dampen my enthusiasm for New Zealand and the wonderful fishing.

We visited several other lodges and fished other streams. We had fine fishing and more companionable guides. We fished one river, the Waiuau, from a jet boat, which was a new experience. A rancher I met gave us a demonstration of a top sheep dog in action. He referred to the dog as a strong-eyed dog. He said it never barked but controlled the sheep with dirty looks. The rancher was very accommodating and sent his dog out into a vast pasture to cut out four sheep and herd them into a corner. It all happened in about as much time as it takes to read this sentence.

Our last stop in New Zealand was Lake Benmore, near Christchurch. An old friend and admirer of Orvis there offered to guide us. He took us up to the shallow end of the lake, where we waded and could see huge browns taking nymphs among the weeds. You had to cast a small nymph very accurately and twitch it as the fish approached. It was a new kind of fly-fishing to me, but I was certainly fascinated. It reminded me, somewhat, of sight casting to bonefish.

So we saw and experienced a lot and had some of the most wonderful trout fishing I had ever enjoyed. Romi and I felt like we had more than enough material for a really first-rate article on New Zealand and its fly-fishing, and then we sat down in our first-class seats for the return trip and opened the in-flight magazine to an article written by C. R. Smith, who was then the chairman of American Airlines. The subject was fly-fishing in New Zealand. When I got back to my office at Orvis, I contacted the American vice president who had arranged our trip and told him how much we had enjoyed ourselves. I then said we were prepared to write an excellent article for his magazine, but that we had noticed this other article, written by the chairman.

The vice president said he was pleased that we had enjoyed ourselves, but it would not be necessary for us to write an article on New Zealand. I'd done a lot of fishing and hunting on my own dime and called it work—or work-related, anyway—but this was a whole new way of doing business. Unfortunately, it never happened again.

Being in the fly-fishing business, I suppose it was predictable that I would spend some time in New Zealand, even if I couldn't find someone to fly me there first class and pay all my expenses. But there are other parts of the world where I have traveled and enjoyed memorable sport that seem less likely places for someone with my kind of interests—India, for instance.

I'd made one brief visit to India back in the days when I was looking for new sources of bamboo. Like a lot of people, I'd been dismayed by the poverty and was happy to leave once I'd finished my business there. I hadn't expected I would ever return. But that was before I became friends with Deep Anand.

Deep is one of eleven children from a well-to-do Hindu family from Pakistan. They lost everything when India became independent from Great Britain and the partition sent the Hindus walking out of Pakistan with nothing but the clothes on their backs while the Muslims were walking in to take over their land. Deep, who was educated in England, vowed to make his family fortune back and went into the automobile-parts business. People in India, as in many poor nations, don't trade in cars the way we do here. They drive them forever, and there is a tremendous demand for replacement parts. Deep had decided to approach the Gabriel Shock Absorber Company about a joint venture in India and showed up at corporate headquarters in Cleveland asking for a meeting with the CEO to talk about it. They tried to give him the brush off, but he wouldn't go away. He kept coming back and knocking on the door until, finally, they agreed to listen to his proposal. This led to a joint venture with Gabriel, which was the first of many that Deep made with other companies, like Purolator. He now has a dozen plants in India.

I met Deep while he was in Cleveland working out the Gabriel partnership. He learned to do what he called "play" with us, which chiefly involved hunting ducks and fishing out at Fritz Neubauer's. Deep evidently spotted me as the most proficient outdoor playboy in our group, and years later, when he was well on his way to industrial and financial success, he invited Romi and me over to India to play with him.

Deep did things in style. We went on a hunting and fly-fishing safari with a staff of nineteen servants and a small semitruck that went in advance so that camp would be ready for us when we arrived at our destination for the night. There was another car for backup.

We fished for several days on the Ramaganga River in Corbett State Park, near the border with Tibet. The park is over five hundred square kilometers of jungle, hills, and grasslands, and it contains the largest concentration of tigers in the world. We never saw a tiger, but we did see tracks on the riverbank. We did see wild elephants, wild boar, pea fowl, jungle cock, and all sorts of other wildlife.

We were fishing for mahseer, which, according to my research, were fine sport and grew to considerable size—up to 120 pounds. They were generally fished for with very heavy-duty tackle—spoons, live bait, plugs—and there wasn't much in the literature about fly-fishing for them. But I wanted to try, in spite of the fact that our host and his friends insisted that fly tackle was no match for the mahseer.

We were staying about forty minutes from the river, and to get there we had to pass through a gate that a guard did not open until sunup. It seemed to me if I was going to experience true early morning fishing—which might well be the best time with a fly—I was going to have to spend the night on the riverbank. I insisted on this, much to the dismay of my Indian friends, who finally provided me with a cot. I didn't accomplish much as an angler, but I did provide some excitement. The next morning my hosts pointed to the tracks of a large male tiger that had approached within forty feet of my bunk during the night. Deep assured Romi that I was perfectly safe since the tigers in that area were prejudiced and didn't like white meat.

The next evening, on another section of the river, I caught my first mahseer. The fish took a brown-and-white bucktail and took out my entire fly line and twenty yards of backing on the first run. The subsequent runs were even stronger, so I was surprised when I brought the fish in and found it weighed only about three pounds. We'd heard that the flesh of the mahseer was highly prized in India so we tried it that night. It was as good as any fish we had ever eaten.

As fine a game fish and food fish as the mahseer is (the English translation of *mahseer* is "mighty tiger"), it seems almost impossible to believe that it is a close relative to the lowly carp. But the large, heavy scales and the two short barbel whiskers confirm this. The resemblance ends there however. The noble mahseer has a far more streamlined shape than the carp—which accounts, no doubt, for the speed of its runs—a beautiful golden hue with pink or orange fins, and an intelligent eye set high in its head, unlike other carp. The mahseer has an unusual mouth, very large with rubbery lips, like a bonefish and ideal for holding a hook. Back in its throat, it has what are called pharyngeal teeth for crushing crabs and other bait. These teeth do quite a job, going by the evidence of mangled spoons and hooks showed to us by spin fishermen.

During the shooting portion of our safari, we were joined by the maharaja of Patiala, who graciously invited us to visit his palace to shoot partridge with him. We took him up on it and were entertained royally—so to speak—by the maharaja and his charming wife, Neti.

Our partridge shoot was in the Punjab province, which is the bread basket of India. The maharaja took us to some mustard fields, where we were joined by five of his friends and some beaters. We split into two parties, with four guns in one and five in the other. Each party was assigned about ten beaters. The beats were mostly short, running through small fields, and each flushed anywhere from one to ten birds. We must have done about fifteen beats and bagged about seventy birds—black partridge, gray partridge, and a few quail. It was a very satisfying and interesting day of shooting.

The history of the maharaja was even more interesting than the shooting. The sort of thing you read in books but never expect to encounter in the flesh. The dynasty's lineage went back to the fourteenth century, and the stories of the palace and the family's power and influence were incredible. Their treasures were breathtaking. The one that sticks in my mind was a set of eight—numbered one through eight—matched Churchill guns that belonged to the maharaja's father. I'm not the sort who ordinarily goes gaga over guns, but eight numbered Churchills, all with matching walnut stocks . . . it was like being exposed to the Hope diamond.

The maharaja and his father were conservative types in that each had only one wife. The grandfather, on the other hand, had had some sixty wives and three hundred concubines, which works out to about one woman for each day of the year. Deep told me that he had gone to school with nine of the man's sons, all the same age and so, obviously, from different mothers. That maharaja's progeny totaled several hundred. If that were not enough of a legend, the story was told of how, when the railroad came to that part of India, he had challenged the train to a race. The maharaja was on horseback, and over a six-hour period he wore out six horses. But he beat the train.

Of the places where I have been for sport, there is one where I have also managed to do quite a bit of business. That, of course, would be England. I made my first visit there in 1970 and was so taken with the rich sporting tradition that I later arranged for Orvis to buy a beat along the Test and one on the Itchen, which were then made available to our customers for a daily fee. (This was part of a larger deal that laid the basis for Orvis U.K.) We also get in a board meeting that includes some fishing on these streams every other year.

On that first trip, I'd gotten yet another reminder of what a rube American I am. Romi and I were picnicking at a fishing hut on the Itchen with the man we had come to visit, Dermot Wilson. He had a little mail-order fly-fishing catalog and ran a small fly-fishing school out of the charming mill at Nether Wallop, part of which dated to the twelfth century. Dermot sold some of our rods and equipment in his catalog. He received us very cordially, and, typically, I had started to think I fit in pretty well. So when he handed me a rod to try, during our picnic on the Itchen, I took it to the bank and started casting without giving much thought to the elaborate traditions of fly-fishing in England, where there are some things a proper angler simply does not do. Not if he is a gentleman, anyway.

I'm a left hander, and from where I was standing, I could cast only downstream. In England, one simply does not fish downstream. There is a complicated reasoning behind this rule, which doesn't really make much sense or much difference. The important thing is—upstream casts only. But I wasn't really fishing—I didn't even have a fly tied on. I was just casting to test the rod Dermot had handed me.

I hadn't been at it long when an irate angler on the neighboring beat came stomping up to remonstrate with me. His name, it turned out, was Commander Armitage, and it fit him perfectly. He drew himself up righteously and lectured me severely for fishing the hallowed Itchen downstream. I tried to explain to the commander that I wasn't really fishing, merely testing a rod, but he just glared at me, like he'd caught me spray-painting graffiti on the walls of Balmoral. Then he turned and marched off, muttering, "Bad form. Bad form, indeed."

Romi concurred with Commander Armitage entirely and still tells that story with obvious delight.

But I wasn't about to let the experience of being called up short over some breach of protocol keep me from that wonderful fishing. In 1983, we were back with our directors. Orvis now owned the mill at Nether Wallop, and my son Perk was running our U.K. operations from there. His wife, Randall, had just given birth to a baby son, my first grandson, and all was well. We even had good fishing. Then, on the Test one day, Romi took a fall and broke her ankle. National Health put her in a cast, gave her a pair of crutches, and sent her on her way.

Usually, in a case like that, you would go home to rest up and recover, but Romi and I had other plans. We were going to Africa. I had been there once, in the sixties, and like everyone who has seen Africa I'd longed to go back. So less than two days after returning to Vermont from England—just long enough to unpack and repack—Romi and I were on our way. She had progressed to a walking cast that she hoped would enable her to get around.

Our first stop was in Johannesburg, South Africa, where we called on our Orvis dealer, Tom Sutcliffe, who had arranged for some bird hunting for us. We flew up to Natal in a small charter—with Tom flying the plane—to an area that looked like Montana. We hunted what they called gray-winged partridge—properly, gray-wing francolin—over bird dogs. They had big, strong English pointers, and the shooting was superb. The birds held and got up in coveys, like Hungarian partridge.

Romi wore the bottom off her walking cast, following those pointers around on foot all day, but that turned out not to be a problem since Tom Sutcliffe was not just an Orvis dealer, he was also an orthopedic surgeon. At the end of the hunt, he said, "We'll just run over to the plaster room and replace your cast." The cost of what Tom called a rugby cast came to about seven dollars; Romi said that it was more comfortable than her previous cast, and it held up through the rest of our safari, through South Africa and Botswana.

At dinner that night, after the fine shoot, I made another typical, bonehead, ugly-American mistake. Our host Bob Mollentze had a fine, strong English pointer, the biggest pointer I had ever seen at a lean eighty pounds. So I complimented him on the dog and remarked that he pointed with a flat tail, much like the pointers in England and unlike the dogs in America, which had been bred for a high tail so that they could be seen in the brush and high grass. I asked, indulgently and probably a little patronizingly, "How long have you had English pointers in South Africa?"

"Longer than you've had them in America," he answered.

Well, I seldom went anywhere without putting my foot in it at least once.

We went from South Africa to Botswana, where we joined up with my sister, Sallie, and her husband and my cousins Rip and Susan McIntosh, whom we met in Victoria Falls. The tent safari in Botswana was everything we could have hoped for, with first-rate service, excellent food, and wonderful big game viewing—we weren't there to shoot them—including sightings of rare species such as kudu and sable. And we had excellent bird shooting for francolin, guinea fowl, sand grouse, five kinds of ducks, and two kinds of doves. We were also accompanied by a naturalist, whose name was Tim Liversedge, and he made everything much more interesting through his commentaries and explanations.

I was having just a grand time and may have gotten a little carried away one evening when we were shooting doves and pigeons. I had shot a particularly handsome pair of large pigeons, and, as is my custom, I had opened their crops to see what they had been eating. In this case, it was a kind of big, white nut that resembled a macadamia. I asked the junior white hunter, who was with me, if they were edible, and he replied, "I guess so. The pigeon ate them."

So I ate two or three and immediately experienced a sharp burning sensation in my stomach that was no ordinary heartburn.

When I got back to camp, I reported to Tim and explained what I'd done.

"My God," he said. "Those nuts are poisonous. When cattle eat them, they die."

This set off the alarm bells. I had a lot more in common with a cow than a pigeon, and we were at least seventy-two hours from medical help, probably farther, since we had no radio communication with anyone who could send help by air and driving in that area was slow business. If you tried to speed, you'd just break an axle.

But Tim was resourceful, and he knew first aid. He filled me up with some very salty water and urged me to vomit just as soon as possible. I didn't need a lot of coaxing at this point and went off into the bush for a little privacy. Well, it was after dark by now, and I was soon interrupted by Tim, who dragged me back, shouting that if the hyenas found me out there—retching and disabled—they might attack.

In the end, I managed to bring up the poison nuts and to avoid having my flesh ripped by hyenas. Now that I had survived my ordeal, it was Romi's turn.

She was still walking around in her cast and was on her way to the privy one night when she tripped over a root and hit her head on a metal ammunition box. She cut her head, and, like most head wounds, it bled copiously. Still, she went on to the privy, stunned from the fall, and, somehow or other, managed to fall through one of the walls, which was made of cement-encrusted burlap and was fairly substantial. She left a lot of blood from her head wound all around the place before retreating to her tent to lie down.

Well, a few minutes later, Susan McIntosh arrived on the scene and assumed the worst. She came screaming back into camp saying that hyenas or a lion had grabbed Romi. We followed her to the privy, and the scene was pretty horrifying. I honestly thought for a minute or two that Susan was right, that there just wasn't any other explanation.

We hadn't been searching long when I heard a moan from our tent and found Romi on her cot, in a pool of blood but, otherwise, none the worse for wear. I patched up the rather nasty gash on her head. It should have had stitches, but all I could manage was some butterfly bandages from tape. But they worked well, and I was proud of my handiwork.

We proceeded with our safari and saw fresh lion kills, charging buffalo, and all the wonders of Africa. But Romi's performance was the highlight that we all remembered and talked about.

I could go on and on. I've been on so many wonderful sporting trips. Romi and I were among the very first anglers to go after bonefish at Christmas Island, in the Pacific, which turned out to be one of the great new sporting destinations in the world. We have hunted dove in Morocco, red-legged partridge in Spain. We've fished in Iceland, Norway, Ireland, Yugoslavia, all over the American West, and in a hundred other places. We've been to Patagonia and to France. In addition to nearly poisoning myself in Africa, I've survived a plane crash in the Bahamas. I've had great sport—caught lots of fish and shot lots of birds—and I've met literally hundreds of wonderful people and manage to stay in touch with many of them and to see some of them on return trips.

If I have learned anything from all these travels, it is that I am just as enthusiastic today about the things that excited me so much when I was a boy. I still love to see a fish take a fly or a bird explode in front of a pointing dog. The difference is that I have a fuller appreciation, now, for the game and the habitat that supports it. I've always been a conservationist, but the more I see of the world, the more dedicated I become to the preservation of the things that I love and think are important.

Chapter 12

Getting Bigger, Getting in Trouble, and Getting Out

In the 1980s Orvis, like the economy as a whole, grew at a robust clip. But the road was not exactly free of potholes. I don't suppose it is for any business. One of the things that happens is that you get cocky, and you think you can do anything. You also forget some of the important lessons you've learned.

Our first serious bump came in the mid-eighties when we acquired a company called Early Winters. At one of our board meetings, I brought up the fact that the Orvis customer wasn't getting any younger, and that the average age of our clothes buyer was in the sixties. Our strategic plan, it seemed to me, should be to find a company that was more youth oriented but had the same outdoor image, in the same field that Orvis was in. We came up with Early Winters, located in Seattle. When it started, Early Winters had the reputation of being a very innovative catalog for backpackers and hikers, with a strong appeal to outdoor-oriented yuppies. The owner and president's main claim to fame came from developing a Gore-Tex backpacker's tent and some unique clothing. He also filled the catalog with a lot of gimmicks, including a portable airplane.

The backpacking and hiking market nosedived as the baby boomers started easing into their forties, and Early Winters began to lean more and more on this gimmicky stuff, which didn't really change its fortunes much. The company was in the first stages of bankruptcy when we were negotiating for them, and I found I was cocky enough to think that with our background of success in mail order Orvis could turn the situation around. I realize now that I should have heeded the advice John Drinko gave me about buying a company that's not making a profit and thinking you're smart enough to turn it around.

Well, we bought Early Winters, and we didn't turn it around. My son Perk was given the job of running it, and I can't fault a thing he did. The company was doomed when we took it over. The experience of trying to turn Early Winters around and then having to take it through bankruptcy was no doubt valuable for a young manager like Perk. But I'm sure it wasn't much fun.

Meanwhile, back at headquarters in Manchester, we were growing so much that we had to make some moves. The most dramatic of these steps was moving the company—or a big part of it, anyway. We had outgrown Manchester, Vermont, which had been home to Orvis for more than one hundred years.

We were warehousing and shipping so much merchandise that we were having a hard time finding enough people to do the work. Manchester didn't have a large labor pool to begin with. And then, the town went through a boom of its own, with all sorts of outlet stores opening up and drawing tourists. They were competing with us for labor and having their own troubles. People were being bused in from an hour away to work in the outlets and at Orvis, but there was still a labor squeeze, and we got into a situation where we had to hire everyone who walked in the door and applied. So we started looking for some place to relocate. Not the corporate headquarters, necessarily, but certainly the warehousing and shipping operations, including the people who took the orders over the phone.

The word got out pretty quickly that Orvis was leaving Vermont. We'd never had very good relations with the state. I think anyone who has tried to run a business in Vermont will tell you that it is a very tough place to do business. The attitude of the people who could help you is indifferent; and on top of that, there are a lot of people who are simply hostile to business. The taxes are high; regulations are tough and complex; and there are a lot of different bureaucracies you have to deal with that don't necessarily talk to each other. We'd never been treated very cordially by the state before we started thinking about leaving, and, while there was some lip service devoted to keeping us there, the follow-through was pretty dismal.

We did consider Bennington, Vermont, a much larger town that was just twenty miles away. It finally came down to a choice between Bennington and Roanoke, Virginia, and the difference was between the states. Virginia gave us a point man who dealt with the five different state bureaucracies we were in contact with; it gave us cash incentives, low taxes for a period of time, money for training our people. A whole package, in other words, whereas Vermont couldn't have been worse. There was no point person, so we had to referee battles between the various state bureaucracies. One would say one thing, and another would say just the opposite. We found it impossible to deal with the state and get a decision. One element that did not tip the scales, interestingly enough, was the cost of labor. The wage rate in Virginia was the same as that in Vermont. This was not the incentive.

The governor of the state, who was Madeline Kunin at that time, did call on me twice, but just about the only reason she could give me for staying in Vermont was that the state had beautiful green mountains and blue skies. I told her that Virginia had pretty much the same color mountains and the same color sky. Her attitude was essentially "How dare you move out of Vermont?"

We had breakfast one morning, just the two of us, and she said, "If you do move your company, what kind of jobs are we talking about losing?"

I said, "Mostly entry-level. Pickers and packers. Telephone operators. Key punchers." I explained that these people were making about a dollar an hour more than minimum wage.

The governor raised herself up and said, "We don't want those starvation jobs in our state."

So we decided to go ahead with the move, and it turned out to be the right decision. We did have a few doubters who wondered how customers would react to someone with a southern accent taking orders for Orvis, a company with a long New England tradition. It didn't worry me, and later on we learned that the southern accents and southern courtesy were tremendous assets. So, in short, the move has been a great success.

But it didn't start out that way. In fact, about three months after the move to Roanoke, I thought we were in serious danger of losing the company. It was probably the most severe crisis at Orvis since I'd bought the company.

The problem was a result of several factors. The first was that I probably delegated too much authority, too fast. We'd been growing so fast that I had a lot of people reporting directly to me. Clayton Shappy drew up one of those organizational charts once, and it went the length of his office wall. This was his way of making the point that I needed to delegate more authority. My boys, who were pretty far up in the hierarchy by then, liked to point out that, on this chart, they were just one line above the chickens that I raised down in Florida for fly-tying feathers.

Eventually, all our key people went off for a couple of days with a consultant to study this matter and to talk about what we were doing and where we were going. This was a free service supplied by IBM, which was very up-front about its belief that if it could make a small company grow into a big company, it would be able to sell that company a lot of equipment. The consultant, who was pretty good, pointed out that I had about twenty-eight people reporting directly to me, which meant that I was still supervising people directly when I should have been supervising their supervisors. It made a lot of sense, and I worked hard on delegating and giving more authority to people who ran the different phases of the business. But I might have been in a little too much of a hurry, especially when you consider how fast the business was both growing and changing and that, on top of all that, we were making a major move. Nevertheless, I turned over a lot of the operational responsibility to one of our bright, able, young managers and made him VP of operations.

The problems began to appear after the move to Roanoke, where we had put in place a new, dynamic, computer-controlled system for filling orders and handling inventory. We started getting complaints—and a lot of them—from customers who were not getting their merchandise or were getting things they hadn't ordered. We were screwing up in just about every way that we could possibly screw things up. I spent a lot of time in Roanoke, trying to get things sorted out, and I was seriously concerned that we might lose the business. I spent a lot of time monitoring people taking orders, and I handled complaints over the phone for a while. I also went down on the floor of the returns department, but the system they had there was so complicated that I figured it would take me a couple of weeks to learn how it worked. So I went back to the programmer, and I said, "Don't you think you could come up with a system that is at least simple enough that the CEO can figure it out?"

He was polite enough not to say, "It depends on the CEO."

After Christmas we were backed up for six weeks with returns from customers who had been shipped the wrong stuff. I did everything from opening boxes to figuring out if the item should go back to stock. I had to get the returns procedure simplified so the person opening the box could make a decision and we could get on with it. Meanwhile, we had as many as nine programmers working full time trying to get the system simplified and straightened out.

When I was on the phone answering complaints, I rarely identified myself as CEO of the company because I wanted our customers to think that whoever they got on the phone was in a position to help fix their problem. I didn't want them to think they had to call the CEO. I learned a lot from that experience, and I was amazed at the tolerance of people once you explained things to them and said, "You're right; we're wrong."

We finally got the problems solved, but it was a nervous time. On the bright side, I learned a lot about our customers and customer service. I also came away from the experience with the knowledge that it is possible to delegate too much too quickly. And I was reminded of something that I had known for a long time. It is the people on the floor who make the system work. If you make it so complex and sophisticated that the foreman can't understand it, tweak it, and jury-rig it so it will run, then you are going to be in trouble. That's exactly the situation we found ourselves in that Christmas, and we paid a price. We had a new system and also a new staff and were able to move only three supervisory people down to Virginia from Vermont. If we'd had our old fulfillment staff on hand, we would have been able to solve a lot of those problems much sooner. It reminded me of what I learned from Russo, the foreman who taught me so much back when I was working in the mines: a good, hands-on foreman can make even an imperfect system work.

So it isn't always enough to learn lessons. You have to remember them, too.

The unfortunate experience with Early Winters and the problems with the move to Roanoke were bumps on a road where the trip was, otherwise, pretty smooth and very exciting. Orvis was becoming a mature company but not a dull one or one that had lost its taste for innovation or its ability to grow.

Orvis U.K. was established in 1982, when our friend in England, Dermot Wilson, got in some financial difficulty and had to sell his little fly-fishing emporium, Nether Wallop Mill. I discussed the potential purchase for Orvis with our directors, pointing out that I wasn't sure it would be a great profit center, but it had real charm and would add sizzle to our image and reputation.

Nether Wallop Mill consisted of an old mill house, parts of which went back to the twelfth century. It was located in the pretty little village of Nether Wallop, near Stockbridge in Hampshire. The mail-order business was conducted out of the mill, as was the inventory and shipping of products. The additional assets that we purchased included those beats on the Test and Itchen Rivers, the two most famous chalk streams in England. The questionable asset was the fly-fishing mail-order business. But we thought we knew how to fix this. Unlike the experience with Early Winters, we knew what we were doing and we had a plan for developing an Anglophile Orvis for the U.K. market. Perk went over to run the U.K. operation, which has thrived. It now consists of fishing schools, leasing of the Test and Itchen beats, and mail order, which has increased many-fold and currently runs about $8 million. The operation includes five stores, one of them in London, and a number of tackle dealers with total sales of more than $12 million, which isn't bad for a Yank outfit.

Another innovation occurred in 1986, while we were preparing the move to Roanoke, with something called the Orvis ELOG program, which has been very successful. It started, the way things usually do, with someone who had an idea and the personality and drive to bring it off. In this case, that person was Vern Bressler, who was one of my greatest friends, a wonderful character, and someone I considered it a privilege to know.

Vern was a third-generation cowboy from Wyoming who had gone to graduate school and become a fisheries biologist by trade. He operated fly-fishing lodges and for some time had been running a place called Rivermeadows, which was a fly-fishing dude ranch in Wilson, Wyoming. He was also involved with two other fly-fishing dude ranches—Three Rivers near Ashton, Idaho, and Firehole, just outside of West Yellowstone, Montana. He was a busy man, but he liked it. In fact, I think he wouldn't have minded being even busier.

Rivermeadows was owned by a Southern California entrepreneur, and Vern discovered very early on that the Hollywood crowd really wasn't cut out for the kind of fly-fishing operation he had in mind. They wanted more frills than fishing. On the other hand, the Orvis mailing list would be a perfect source for the kind of clients he was looking for. I met him on a visit Romi and I had taken to Rivermeadows and written up for the *Orvis News* in 1972 and that immediately booked the whole place for Vern. He was happy with the new class of paying clients Orvis was providing for his ranch, and it was a nice relationship.

In 1985 Vern decided to make a career change, and he came to talk to me about an idea he had. He convinced me that there was a big market for top-quality fly-fishing dude ranches and that Orvis had the mailing list (and the reputation) to fill them with customers. He would find the destinations and put together the right kind of programs throughout the country.

Now, in my experience, most concept people are not the same people you want when it comes time to get the job done. There is a big difference between the idea and the execution. Good implementers are a different breed of cat and rarer, most of the time, than the concept people. But Vern was one of those unusual people who was both an idea man and an excellent implementer. When he said he could do it, I was positive he could. In January of 1986, we advertised two lodges, Rivermeadows and Three Rivers Ranch, and two outfitters, Bressler Outfitters and Montana Troutfitters. The difference was that while lodges put you up and fed you, the outfitters provided only guided fishing on a daily basis. The response was positive and immediate. This was the beginning of what was expanded to become the Orvis ELOG service, which stood for Endorsed Lodge, Outfitter, and Guide.

The way it worked was that Orvis advertised the ELOG members in its catalog and in the *Orvis News*. The ELOG members paid Orvis a flat fee for the service and took their own reservations. The lodges were required to run an Orvis tackle shop, and the guides were required to have Orvis equipment in their boats and to fish with Orvis equipment. I must admit I was a little dubious at first because most lodges, guides, and outfitters are a pretty independent lot. I didn't realize what Vern did, which was that the lodge owners really wanted some kind of endorsement of quality to separate themselves from the many slipshod, fly-by-night outfits and that to obtain such an endorsement, they would do what it took to make themselves into first-class operations . . . and to get those Orvis bookings.

The program has been a tremendous success, and today we have more than one hundred and fifty lodges, outfitters, and guides enrolled in the program. A very nice side benefit for Orvis is the way we have been established as the premier source of fly-fishing equipment in the Rocky Mountain area.

An interesting note on the ELOG program is that Vern eventually reported to my son Dave, who had worked as a fishing guide for two summers at Rivermeadows in Wyoming back when he was a college student. Vern had been his boss.

One day when Vern was sitting in my office, he said, "You know, back when Dave was working for me, he showed up with a beard, and I made him shave it off. Now that I'm working for him, the beard is back." Not for long, though.

Sadly, Vern died in 1995. But he had turned the business over to his very capable son, Mark, and it is growing even faster under Mark's guidance. In his eulogy to his father at Vern's funeral, Mark quoted his dad's most valuable advice to him: "The more people you like, the happier you will be in this life." I couldn't agree more.

As far as the ELOG goes, it remains a very successful and important part of the business. I've had friends tell me, many times, about their great experiences at Orvis-endorsed lodges and conclude by saying, "If it isn't Orvis endorsed, I'm not going." I don't argue with them.

While we were getting into new things—like ELOG—and moving to new locations, like Roanoke, in the late eighties, that didn't mean we weren't paying attention to the basics. The core of Orvis has always been fly-fishing, and the soul of fly-fishing has always been the fly rod. A lot of successful companies get into trouble when they stop paying attention to the basics of what made them successful in the first place. Twenty years after I took over the company, we were as committed as ever at Orvis to making quality fly rods.

In fact, it seemed to me that the revolution in rod-building materials and technology had given us an opportunity to push the envelope a little bit. We might just be able to make the kind of rods that, up until now, anglers had only dreamed about because it was simply impossible to build them. I was thinking, specifically, of very light rods.

Most anglers are attracted to the idea of lighter, finer, more delicate tackle. There is something appealing about using the very lightest rod possible, with a very small fly and a leader that looks like sewing thread and tests at about one-pound breaking strength. Using tackle like that requires more skill and touch on the part of the angler and makes the contest more equal, especially when you are going after big fish. Also, trout feed on a lot of tiny insects that are imitated by flies so small that you need delicate tackle—fine leaders, especially—to fool them. And, finally, there is just something in all of us that wants to minimize the equipment in any experience. You want to go in with the very least you can get by with. Anything more seems like an encumbrance and detracts from the purity of the experience.

Actually, I like fine tippets and one- and two-weight rods for trout fishing because it is a more practical and efficient way to fish. When large trout are feeding on small flies on spring creeks, you need to be able to deliver a very small fly—#18 or #20 or even smaller—on a 6× or 7× tippet (which translates into diameters of .005 and .004 inches, respectively) with as little disturbance as possible. This can be done best with the delicate rods designed for one- and two-weight lines. Once a trout is hooked, the super-light rod acts as a sensitive shock absorber to protect the light tippet. There is also the fact that when you are fishing with a one-weight rod, even a nine-inch trout feels like a monster.

The challenge with fly tackle had always been in the materials you used to build rods. Without getting too technical, in fly-fishing the weight of the line imparts action to the rod, and at some point you couldn't get any lighter because the rod-making material—bamboo—just couldn't be made any finer without becoming too fragile. Using the modern system of grading fly lines, a three-weight was about as low as you could go before the rod just got too fragile to be practical.

In bamboo, the six-weight was the traditional all-purpose trout rod. A lot of anglers liked a five-weight, and the four-weight was popular, especially with the anglers who liked to go light. Orvis had made a seven-foot bamboo rod for a three-weight line, and it sold, but it was a challenge to cast. When graphite came along, most trout fishermen began to move to light rods, in four- and five-weights—also three-weights, which was as light as fly lines were made. (When we went to these new rods, we had to work with the line companies to come up with the right tapers for the lines.)

But graphite was so much stronger than bamboo that it seemed to me you could come up with a taper that would cast an even lighter line. If you could, then you would have a product that would move along with an obvious trend in fly-fishing toward smaller flies, more delicate leaders, and generally lighter tackle all around.

So I went to Howard Steere, and we talked about it. Howard was the same can-do guy he'd always been, and he went right to work and came out with the first production rod for a two-weight line. And it was no gimmick. The rod had terrific action. I took one of the prototypes with me on a trip out west and used it on the Railroad Ranch section of the Henry's Fork—one of the finest, most demanding trout streams in the world—to take a twenty-four-inch rainbow trout on a tiny, #24 dry fly and a 7x leader tippet. This was about as fine as you could go at the time. I was sold, and so were a lot of other anglers.

Then, in 1987, we topped that. We came out with the one-weight rod. A one-weight line is 30 percent lighter than the two-weight, quite a dramatic difference. I tested that rod on the Malleo River in Argentina in late March, when the red stags were bugling in the hills and the geese were gathering to migrate—a truly wonderful time of year on one of my favorite rivers in the world. I took a fine rainbow on my third cast and then, a little later, another fish that went twenty-two inches. Quite a baptism for that little rod. Later, on that same trip, I took the one-weight to the Rio Grande (the one near Esquel, Argentina, not to be confused with the Reo Grande in Tierra del Fuego), which has some of the strongest fish in the world, and landed a fish that I estimated at seven pounds. The rod acted as a shock absorber so the fish could not break my fine tippet, and I honestly believe that I landed it more quickly than I could have with a conventional six-weight rod. The one-weight also caught on with a certain kind of Orvis customer, and those customers were so passionate about the rod that we started an Orvis one-weight club, where people could write in to the *News* with stories about the big fish they caught on this nifty little rod.

We went one step further then and made a one-ounce rod. Fly rods for trout had generally been in the three- to four-ounce range, as far as weight of the rod goes—even that can begin to feel like a lot if you are casting all day. Once again, anglers wanted more from less, and we gave it to them with the one-ounce rod. One of the best rods in this series handles a four-weight line, and with this rod, believe me, you can do just about anything you can do with a traditional trout rod—and more. My son Perk even caught a bonefish on one of these rods.

These light rods were something new and innovative, so, naturally, they stirred up a little controversy. Some people went so far as to say that they were cruel to the fish, requiring a longer fight so that, at the end, the fish was too exhausted to recover. But those people had it exactly backwards. The lighter rods allowed the angler to put more pressure on the fish—without fear of breaking a light tippet—so that it could be brought to hand, and released, more quickly. I think most good anglers came to this conclusion pretty quickly. I use the one-weight on my spring creeks in Wyoming, where I regularly catch rainbow, brown, and cutthroat trout over twenty inches and release them unharmed. As anyone who owns or leases a spring creek will tell you, the last thing you are interested in doing is killing the fish that live there. You are extremely protective of your trophy trout. If I thought that light-line rods were in any way detrimental to the health of the trout, I not only wouldn't use them, I'd be in favor of outlawing them. Orvis one- and two-weight rods are fine angling tools, another great Orvis innovation.

So when it came to fly rods, Orvis was still where I wanted it to be at the end of the eighties—leading the way. The foundation of the company has always been the design and building of quality fly rods, so it was gratifying when in 1989 Tom Peters, the author of *In Search of Excellence*, named the Orvis fly rod as the best product made in the United States in the eighties. We knew we made something special, and anglers all around the world knew it. But it was nice to have it reported in *USA Today* by someone with the authority of Peters.

Orvis had obviously grown and prospered since I bought it, and I was certainly pleased and even a little surprised. I expected the company would grow. I certainly wanted it to grow. But I don't think I ever expected it would grow quite as fast as it did.

Virtually all of this growth had come from inside. We expanded on our own core business, and when we found new areas to get into, we did it on our own. We hadn't done much in the way of acquisitions, except for Early Winters, and maybe that experience soured us a little, though Orvis U.K. was also an acquisition and certainly a success. The acquisition route is a fairly dramatic way to go, and you've almost always got problems with fit. Also, we had set up a strong criterion at Orvis regarding acquisitions: we would consider only companies that would enhance our reputation for quality in the fields of fly-fishing, bird hunting, and country living. This narrowed the field considerably.

The Gokey Boot Company was a perfect fit, if you'll pardon the pun. It was almost the same age as Orvis—Noah Gokey started making boots in 1850—and it also had a reputation among sportsmen for making quality products. Gokey was to hunting boots what Orvis was to fly rods.

I had known about—and worn—Gokey boots since I was about ten years old. In fact, my father had worn Gokey boots quail hunting virtually all his life, and when he was seventy years old, he decided he needed a new pair of Gokey's famous snake-proof boots for hunting quail at his place in Georgia. He knew from experience that no matter how many hunting years he had left, those boots were going to outlast him. So he got them made a half size too large so they would fit my feet, and when he died, six years later, in 1963, they became mine. I wore them for twenty years and then turned them over to my son Dave, who wore them for several more years.

I had gone to the Gokey company in my early Orvis days with my scheme for trading mailing lists and during my visit had mentioned something about the possibility of a merger. They laughed me off, saying that maybe Gokey would buy Orvis, since they were three times larger than we were.

But those numbers changed fairly radically, especially after Gokey was bought out by a company that acquired small mail-order outfits. The Gokey company was in a pretty advanced state of decline by the late eighties, losing about a million dollars a year on a volume of three million. The boot business hadn't grown much, and while Gokey made and marketed very good canvas and leather luggage, Orvis sold a similar product, and all the marketing momentum was with our name. But I believed in their boots and still do. A lot of boots these days are built out of synthetics and are advertised as being rugged, waterproof, and the last word in high-tech sophistication, but I don't think any boot can compare to a hand-stitched, moccasin-construction, all-leather Gokey for sheer comfort in the field—and when you get right down to it, that is what you want in a boot, something that doesn't hurt your feet and actually feels good on them. I spend a lot of time walking behind bird dogs in the woods, and I just like the way Gokey boots feel on my feet and often don't take them off until bedtime. I once said to a friend of mine, on a wet afternoon in Vermont, that I'm more comfortable in a pair of damp Gokeys than I would be in any other boot bone dry.

Buying Gokey, then, made good sense. No question about that. It would have been the right move, even if there hadn't been a sentimental attachment. And once we had made that acquisition, others began to seem logical. Our next big move along those lines came in 1993 when we bought British Fly Reel. The ball got rolling one evening on the Test River when I was fishing with my old friend Barrie Welham of Hampshire. Barrie was, to me, the number-one guy in fly-fishing in the U.K. He had started with the Hardy Company as one of their tournament casters and a top salesman and had gone on to introduce several U.S. companies to the U.K., including Gladding and, later, Scientific Anglers. And he had developed British Fly Reel. With his staff, we had designed several reels for Orvis, including our Battenkill and Madison models. He also manufactured reels for Scientific Anglers and Cortland, which were competitors of Orvis. They had been bigger than we were when I acquired Orvis, but we had long since overtaken them by the time Barrie and I had our little conversation on the Test.

British Fly Reel was the largest manufacturer in the world for fly reels over twenty-five dollars, but there were problems, and in his direct, almost blunt way, Barrie suggested that Orvis ought to buy the company. A British holding company had acquired British Fly Reel, he explained as we sat on a bench beside the river, and under its management, we could expect the quality of our reels to go down, since the company was not reinvesting in the necessary tooling. This got my attention since one of my firm mandates was that Orvis never offer anything that was not of top quality. Also, I liked the idea of getting into the manufacturing of our own product. I have always believed that the best way to insure quality is to make the product yourself.

Barrie and I didn't do much fishing that evening, even though there were trout rising. We talked over all the potential problems, including the fact that if we did buy British Fly Reel, it might jeopardize the company's relationship with its second and third largest customers, Scientific Anglers and Cortland. This didn't bother me too much, since Orvis was getting its fly lines made by those companies. We might as well make their reels. By the end of the day, I was convinced, and, eventually, Orvis acquired British Fly

Reel, with Barrie Welham and John Gall, the works manager, as part owners and partners, so we had the right men to run the company, which was an enormous asset. British Fly Reel has been a successful profit center. Buying this company gave us what is called vertical integration and afforded us much more control over the manufacturing of our own reels. It also meant that we were now selling reels to some of the companies that had been our much larger competitors when I'd bought Orvis and we were in the position of having to take whatever reels our supplier was willing to let us have. It also made Orvis the largest manufacturer of quality fly reels in the world.

The next acquisition was a venerable old shooting preserve outside of Millbrook, New York, called Sandanona. Although it held the first shooting preserve license issued in the United States, Sandanona was having trouble making it, even though it was on a beautiful piece of ground, not far from New York City and Westchester County, where a lot of sportsmen and potential customers for an upscale shooting operation worked and lived. Don Kendall, the former CEO of Pepsi, who is an Orvis director, knew Sandanona and thought it would be a good investment and a natural fit for us. I agreed with him, but, by this time, it wasn't my call. I was still chairman of Orvis, but there was a new CEO, my son Perk, and perhaps because of his experience with Early Winters, he was reluctant to buy Sandanona. Finally, Kendall said, "Well, if you won't buy it, I will," which was a lot like what John Drinko had said to me when we were negotiating with Duckie Corkran to buy Orvis. That gave Perk the push he needed, and Sandanona became Orvis Sandanona and a great success under Dave Perkins's management. With the continuing boom on Wall Street, more and more young people with money are curious about the sporting life. They want to know what it is like to shoot a shotgun—either at a clay target or a live pheasant—and they are in the habit of buying brand names they know and trust. Orvis is one of those names, so when they want to sample the sporting experience, they come to Sandanona. And, frequently, they come back again and again.

The addition of Sandanona—and the other acquisitions—was an important event for the company and, of course, for me. But the big story of the nineties has been the changing of the guard—for the company and certainly for me.

I can't say that I ever got tired of running Orvis. Like a lot of chief executives, I had times when I'd be awfully tired of the personnel problems—that's unavoidable and comes with the terrain. But I never lost my enthusiasm for the business. And I still haven't.

But ... it had always been my intention, from the time I bought the company, to make Orvis into a two- or even a three-generation family business. My children clearly enjoyed doing the same things I liked to do, and I was convinced, even when they were young, that my boys would be capable of running the business once I'd stepped down.

I discussed the matter with Perk and his younger brother (by three years) Dave while they were both in college. I still wanted them in the business, and Dave was game. But Perk had some reservations and understandably so. All college students should be idealists, and Perk was every bit of that. His cause was the environment, and he was considering going to law school and then going out and becoming an environmental lawyer. I told him I understood his feelings but that he might find himself in a far better position to help the environment from the platform of a successful businessman than as just another flag waver and mouthpiece. I believe he took my advice under serious consideration.

But first he and his college roommate took a trip around the world. They traveled by jeep most of the places they went, booking passage from Brazil to Amsterdam, for instance, on a ship where the jeep went along in the cargo hold. They used the same method to tour most of Europe, Asia, and Australia, and, while

Perk came down pretty seriously ill on two occasions, they made it home all right and had a genuinely memorable experience.

When he got home, Perk told me that if he'd ever had any inclination toward becoming an international bum, he'd gotten over it on that trip. He had run into a number of specimens of the breed and found most of them aimless and unhappy. This recalled for me my own father's advice that very few people are intelligent enough to live a happy life without the discipline of a job. Perk went to work at Orvis in 1977, replacing Baird Hall, who had retired as editor of the *Orvis News*. It was a tough act to follow, but Perk did it very well.

After he'd worked at that job for a while, Perk moved to San Francisco—first to find a location for an Orvis store, then to open it and run it. We wanted to establish a presence on the West Coast to counter the image we had of being an old-line, eastern outfit. Perk found an ideal, offbeat location on Maiden Lane where you had to walk down several steps to get to the entrance of the store. He had a rock garden that included a stream that held live trout designed for the entrance. The rock garden became home to one of the many San Francisco street people, but he was usually out of sight by opening hours. One Christmas Eve he slipped a card under the door, addressed to all the people of Orvis, and signed it "The Orvis Bum." That's class.

Perk married his wife, Randall, while he was in San Francisco, and then the two of them moved to Nether Wallop Mill in England to run Orvis U.K. My first grandson, Simon, was born there. From England, Perk went on to Seattle and the Early Winters experience.

After Seattle, Perk returned to Vermont and took over the mail-order division of Orvis, which accounts for about 70 percent of the company's business. He was vice president, then president of the company, and, in 1992, succeeded me as CEO.

It was my idea. But I wanted Perk to set the timetable, and he did. He was probably a little less hasty about it than I expected.

I later learned that one of the reasons he wasn't in a bigger hurry to send me off to pasture was his concern for how things would work out with his brother, Dave, under the new regime. The boys had always been close, and it was one thing when they were both working for the old man. But once Perk became CEO, that would change, and Perk wasn't sure how he felt about that—or, more importantly, how his brother felt about it.

Dave had been working at Orvis since 1979, and he certainly knew his way around the company. He'd started as a cashier in the basement sale room, right after he graduated from college, so he learned the business from the bottom up—literally. At twenty he was manning the cash register, and from there he moved upstairs and ran the Orvis store, which was our only retail outlet in those days. His next experience was recruiting dealers, and this would be invaluable for Dave as he went on to take over the fishing and shooting schools before going down to Houston to locate and run our second off-premises retail operation. He came back after that and ran the dealer department and took over more and more responsibility for retail, finding locations for stores in New York, Houston, Dallas, Atlanta, and other cities and then recruiting and training the people to run those stores. Eventually, he oversaw all Orvis retail, which, with the dealers, accounts for about 30 percent of Orvis's gross sales. Dave always did a fine job and I never had any doubts about his ability to take on the next challenge. Evidently, however, he wasn't quite so sure himself. I heard from a friend, later on, that Dave once said, "You know, I think that all along Dad had more confidence in me than I did. And, of course, that gave me confidence."

I didn't know this at the time, but when Perk was trying to come up with a timetable for assuming leadership of the company, he went to Dave and asked him how he would feel about it. Would it change their relationship if his brother became his boss?

What Dave said, I'm told, is, "Hey, great. It'll be a lot more fun working for you than for Dad."

* * *

I've written a lot about my sons here, but I should also say something about the three daughters who are the delights of my life and have also played their parts in the Orvis story.

My oldest daughter, Molly, worked in the San Francisco store for Perk and later as an assistant buyer in Vermont. One day she came to me and said, "I am fed up with being bossed around by my father and two brothers. I quit."

I replied, "I don't blame you. There is such a thing as too much family in a business, especially if you are at the bottom of the totem pole."

Molly went back to school and became a veterinary technician. But she had retailing in her blood, so after working a couple of years as a vet's assistant, she spoke to her brother Dave and said she would like to build an Orvis dealership in Chagrin Falls, Ohio, the suburb of Cleveland, where she lived. This time, she explained, she would be the customer (therefore the boss) and could give her brothers orders.

With very little help from her brothers or her father, she built a very successful business and became one of the largest independent Orvis dealers. She runs her own fishing school in conjunction with the store, which is not surprising since she is an excellent wing shot and fly fisher.

Our youngest daughter, Melissa, is also an extremely keen fly fisher, since she took most of her spring vacations as a teenager fishing with her mother and me. Melissa fell in love with Argentina and took her husband, Sean, there on their honeymoon. He has become an excellent wing shot, but Melissa still beats him fly-fishing, especially on the difficult spring creeks.

I remember one time when they were taking turns casting to a big, rising trout at our Wyoming place. It was her turn to fish, while Sean was supposed to be watching their eight-month-old firstborn. Just as Melissa's fly—a pale morning dun, I think—was about to reach the fish, Spencer, the baby, crawled past her and completely submerged himself in the creek. I was watching all this and was very proud to see Melissa set the hook in the rising trout before retrieving my submerged grandson with her left hand. That is a real sense of priorities.

Penny, who is Romi's oldest daughter, is the brightest of the lot. She teaches a writing course at Northwestern University and is the drama and movie critic for *Chicago* magazine. But she has used her talents to make a contribution to Orvis, most notably in the form of a poem that rhymed the names of forty different flies. We published the poem in the catalog, and it was a big hit.

And, of course, in discussing various contributions to what is, after all, a family business, there is no way to overlook what Romi has meant to Orvis. I could write another book on that. We still go to gift shows together to come up with ideas for developing new Orvis products, and she is easily the more creative of the two of us. Among all her other talents, she has a great eye. My favorite of all her many contributions to the Orvis story is probably her cookbook, *Game in Season*. Eating wild game is one of the great pleasures of my life and all of Romi's recipes are just terrific. Nick Lyons published the book, which we sell in stores and through the catalog, and it is now in its third printing. Romi is revising and updating it, which is more of my good luck, since she tests every recipe on me.

Perk still calls on Romi for decorating help in the new Orvis offices. Romi has a real knack for this; we even rented her out as a decorator once. It came totally out of the blue. I happened to be walking past the order desks one day when one of the fishing-school instructors, who was filling in on the phones, stopped me and said he'd had a funny inquiry. Some guy in Texas had called and asked if we had an interior decorating service. He went on to say that he was building a new, fancy duck club to entertain his company's customers and he wanted it all decked out in Orvis-type stuff.

I said, "So what did you tell him?"

"I told him we don't have a decorating service."

"Well call him back," I said, "and tell him we just started one. Romi can handle that job."

Sure enough, they signed Romi up and they couldn't have gotten a better decorator. The duck club was near Beaumont, Texas (on Big Hill Road, elevation fourteen feet), and was it ever fancy. It had an elevator and ten bedrooms. Romi decorated each room in the pattern of a different duck—teal, pintail, mallard, and so forth. The bedspreads, lamps, everything in the teal room had teal on it except the toilet seat. She did a great job and they were very pleased. She also got invited on some great duck hunts along with Dave, who was running the Houston store at the time. They both shot speckled belly geese there, something I have never done.

After Perk's conversation with Dave, it was time, and in November of 1992, at the age of sixty-five, I turned Orvis over to my son. Perk gave me a surprise retirement party at the Orvis headquarters in Manchester and invited many of the Roanoke staff people, the store managers, many of our major suppliers, my relatives, and close friends. Instead of the usual roast, he had a spoof of the *Orvis News* printed up that included pictures of me in various embarrassing situations and the story of how in my first dealings with Orvis, when I was an undergraduate at Williams, I had paid for a sixty-five-dollar Battenkill rod with a check that bounced. The party was a marvelous and gentle way of saying to the staff that the old man was going out to pasture.

And I made a point of getting out, too, just like I'd done with Duckie. You don't want the old bull hanging around, butting in all the time. For one thing, personnel will try to find a way to get around the new guy if they think the old guy is still making the decisions. It makes for real unhappy, inefficient management.

I'd have to say the transition has gone very well. You'd like to think that you'll be missed, and you certainly don't want your business to suffer, but since 1992 the boys have more than doubled the business, from $95 million to $200 million. And a higher percentage of that is bottom line than in the days of my leadership.

I'm very proud and, I think, justifiably so.

Chapter 13

Out to Pasture . . .
But Wow, What a Pasture

I'm often asked if I miss running the Orvis company. Of course I miss it—it was my life for twenty-seven years, and my work and my recreation were almost indivisible. I enjoyed making decisions and experiencing the results, which were sometimes disappointing but mostly satisfying. But I have been put out to a nice pasture with plenty of birds, fish, dogs, and grandchildren to play with. And now there is a lot more time for the kind of charitable, philanthropic work I've always been involved in, especially those kinds of projects and organizations that have preservation of wildlife and wildlife habitat as their goals.

My father was a dedicated philanthropist who wanted to raise his children in that spirit. With that in mind, he set up the Perkins Charitable Foundation and made his six kids trustees of it. Perkins Charitable has grown many-fold, and a large portion of its donations go to wildlife conservation and education. While this is the main focus of my philanthropic work, I have been involved in projects that aren't devoted to wildlife conservation. One that was especially satisfying was the Cleveland Scholarship Program.

I don't know how Cleveland Scholarship found me, or I found them. I remember attending a meeting in 1969, conducted by Bob Copeland, the founder of the Cleveland Scholarship Program. Bob was director of a law firm at the time, and managing trustee of something called the Markus Foundation, which had as its principal purpose making higher education scholarships available to inner-city youths in Cleveland. Roy Markus was a self-educated man who believed that education was the solution to breaking the stranglehold of poverty and ignorance on generations of inner-city families. As generous as the Markus Foundation was, there was a need for more. This led to Bob Copeland's creation of the Cleveland Scholarship Program. His very simple idea was that the way to help inner-city youths was to identify the motivated kids with leadership potential and try to help them. He believed that college admissions directors were not the ones to select these kids. Every high school principal and teacher can quickly identify the kind of kids he had in mind.

Bob explained to me, when we first started talking, that he had interviewed kids who had this kind of potential at the beginning of their senior year and asked them what they planned to do. Invariably they said they wanted to go on to college, but very few of them made it, in spite of the fact that there were a number of federal and state programs that would provide financial aid for these kids. The fact is, college entrance forms are quite complicated. Loan and grant applications are even more complicated. Kids coming from families without any background in higher education had little chance of sorting their way through the morass of red tape. So the CSP worked as a self-help program, to help these kids through the maze and get them the aid that they needed and that was out there. To do this, the program provided seed money in the amount of sixteen hundred dollars, half of it in the form of a direct grant and the rest as a student loan. In 1969, twenty-seven of the twenty-nine students in the program made it through their first year of college. Of sixty-seven students from the classes of 1966 and 1967, 85 percent completed their college studies.

I liked everything I heard about this organization and developed a tremendous respect for Bob Copeland. I joined the CSP board and helped raise funds. After a few years, the CSP learned that kids needed additional support once they were in college since they usually came from backgrounds where their parents had not been exposed to higher education and were, sometimes, hostile to the whole idea. When social or academic problems inevitably arose, these kids had a tendency to throw in the towel. CSP found it important to have counselors on the college campus to put an arm around these kids' shoulders and pat them on the ass at the appropriate times—and it worked.

In 1991, Cleveland Scholarship Program started an adult learner program. This was targeted at people between twenty and fifty-six years of age who believe that they are at a dead end without education but still are motivated to raise their living standard and that of their families. The success of this program is incredible, with virtually no dropouts and an average grade point average of 3.43.

The most gratifying and rewarding part about being involved in CSP is meeting the finished product—the graduates and the students who are enrolled in the program. They are bright, upbeat, fine citizens and include the current mayor of Cleveland, doctors, White House fellows, airline pilots, lawyers, and business owners. One individual is head of the human resources department of a major Cleveland hospital. He also teaches at a local university and donates his entire teaching salary to CSP. Today there are nineteen clones of CSP in other cities, serving some thirty thousand students annually. A couple of years ago, a study conducted by Brandeis University proclaimed that CSP was "the best of the best of college access programs."

In 1998, CSP awarded almost two million dollars in scholarship assistance to more than seventeen hundred students. CSP students have a dropout rate that is one third the national average.

CSP is one of the most gratifying organizations I've ever worked for and one of the easiest to raise money for. I'm very proud that my daughter Melissa has become a trustee of CSP. For some reason, they've hung the title of trustee emeritus on me, now that I'm out to pasture. I think it means that you don't have to come to meetings but that you'd better damn well keep raising money.

On the more familiar ground of wildlife and wildlife habitat preservation, in 1985 I created the Orvis-Perkins Foundation, funded

by Orvis, my children, and myself. Orvis-Perkins, which will receive a good bit of my estate, donates almost entirely to conservation programs. And then, early in my ownership of Orvis, we set a
policy of donating 5 percent of pretax profits to fish and wildlife
conservation. In time, we were making substantial contributions
to Trout Unlimited, the Ruffed Grouse Society, The Nature Conservancy, the Atlantic Salmon Federation, and Ducks Unlimited.
In addition to direct contributions, we used space in catalogs and
the *Orvis News* to describe special conservation projects such as The
Nature Conservancy's protection of the South Fork of the Snake
River or Trout Unlimited's restoration of the Blackfoot in Montana.
That Blackfoot project, for example, raised over $200,000. When
we undertook it, we described the problem to our customers and
then advised them that the solution was—money. We promised
to match their contributions and advised them that the National
Fish and Wildlife Foundation would also provide matching money,
which worked out to a three-to-one multiple on their gift. This
gives the individual a sense that his contribution will really make
a difference. It was certainly true in this case, and our customers thanked us. I personally got involved in a lot of these efforts
when I was still running Orvis, and there was always a sense of
satisfaction in giving something back.

When I took over Orvis, people in the field of conservation sought
me out. The first of the organizations that came calling was Trout
Unlimited, and I agreed to serve on the board. It would become one
of the less successful, and more frustrating, of my conservation efforts. TU was very good at the local level—informing people about
and leading the opposition to a new dam, say—but it wasn't very good
at coming up with a comprehensive, national agenda. This was understandable, since rivers are unique and have individual problems.
    The low point in my association with Trout Unlimited came
at an annual membership meeting. The executive director of TU
had trouble getting a clear message from the board regarding its
mission and the direction of the organization. This resulted, pre-

dictably, in a lot of turnover at the top position. At this particular meeting, we were scheduled to be addressed by yet another new executive director. When it came time for the man to speak, he took the microphone and proceeded to lambaste the board with a very liberal use of four-letter words. He was just getting started on what he thought of the membership, when a couple of the largest board members grabbed him by the elbows and removed him from his position on the dais—and from his position as executive director. The board members noted that this was a record, even at Trout Unlimited, for the shortest executive directorship.

I should mention that my son Perk joined the board of Trout Unlimited well after my term was up, and I am sure he was a far more effective board member than I was. Trout Unlimited has matured since my time there and is an effective outfit today.

The second organization I became personally involved with was the Ruffed Grouse Society, where I served on the board and as president—and met Gordon Guillion, who was a wonderful naturalist and biologist. Just about the finest sport we have in Vermont is grouse hunting, which lasts from the last weekend in September until the middle of November, when deer season comes on. This is the time when the leaves are turning and the weather is changing, and the hills of Vermont are red and gold and as beautiful as any place on earth.

I believe almost everyone who loves hunting and fishing eventually reaches the stage where he becomes more interested in preserving habitat than he is in taking the game, and Gordon gave me an education in grouse and their habitat.

While he was familiar with most of the grouse species, Gordon's specialty was ruffed grouse and woodcock and the early successional forests that were their primary habitat. Most of his research, as it turned out, had been done in the area around Cloquet, Minnesota, where I had done my hunting when I was working in the mines, so we began our friendship with a lot to talk about.

Before Gordon came along, the focus of the Ruffed Grouse Society was on limits, seasons, and predator control as a way to keep the populations up. Gordon's research proved that the real key was good habitat, the most critical of which was the early successional forests, and that the principal tree was the aspen. Good aspen habitat almost inevitably meant good grouse populations and good hunting. Aspen requires clear-cutting for regeneration, and, as Gordon's research established, the grouse depends on the aspen in three stages of maturity.

In the early stage, there is high stem density. Straight vertical stems make ideal brood habitat and good cover against predators—both birds and mammals. Midlife aspen, when stems are three to six inches in diameter, is ideal during the fall hunting season, as there is often a diversity of food and still good cover for escaping predators. There is enough shading that there is not a lot of lateral ground cover for mammalian predators to hide in, but the cover is still dense enough that goshawks, which are real grouse killers, can't work their way through it efficiently. In its final, mature stage, the aspen produces high-protein buds, which are the grouse's favorite forage during the winter. The stems of these trees are thick and rigid enough to support a grouse's weight, so a bird can fill its crop quickly on aspen buds and get back into cover, avoiding avian predators.

In addition to establishing all this, Gordon went on to explore the causes of something that had long been a mystery to grouse hunters, including me. About every ten years, there is a crash in the grouse population, followed by a long, slow buildup. There were all sorts of theories to account for this, most of them not very scientific. People linked this crash to everything from increased sunspot activity to shifts in the jet stream—everything, it seemed, except the length of women's skirts. But none of the theories really stood up to scientific scrutiny.

Gordon's theory—which I believe in because I have witnessed it—is that about once every ten years there is a caterpillar attack on aspen. They denude the tree for two or three years before the aspen develops a defensive toxin and the caterpillar can no longer eat the leaves. But this toxin also makes the aspen buds unpalatable to grouse, requiring them to switch to lesser foods such as witch hazel, birch, and ironwood. The grouse are in the open a long time while they are feeding on these much smaller buds, and, because they are perched on flimsy stems, they are doing a lot of flapping around. This activity can go on for a couple of hours, instead of the ten or fifteen minutes it would take to feed in aspen. Grouse are vulnerable, especially to the goshawk and great horned owl, under these conditions, and the populations suffer accordingly.

I might never have gotten such a thorough education in the biology of the ruffed grouse if it hadn't been for my association with the Ruffed Grouse Society. And I might never have met Gordon Guillion, who was a good friend as well as a teacher.

I've met a number of other interesting and effective people through a mutual interest in conservation and other philanthropic work. When I got the American Museum of Fly Fishing started, I was working with Arnold Gingrich, who was the publisher of *Esquire* magazine and had been friends with Ernest Hemingway. In my work with The Nature Conservancy, I was associated with General Norman Schwarzkopf. I served on the board of governors of The Nature Conservancy with John Smale, who was the CEO of Procter & Gamble and later chairman of General Motors. I was so impressed with one chairman of TNC's board, Joe Williams of the Williams Companies, that I asked him to come on the Orvis board, and, happily, he accepted. One of the most valuable contributions I made to TNC was persuading them to make Bob Mitchell, from the Orvis board, a member of TNC's board. Bob straightened out TNC's antiquated and ineffective finance and accounting departments, which is no small contribution to an organization with over a billion dollars in assets.

While I have been involved in all sorts of projects since I left Orvis, I would say that the work I've done with The Nature Conservancy has been as satisfying as anything I've done in the field of conservation. The organization appeals to me because it is apolitical. It stays focused on its objective, which is preserving vital

ecosystems and wildlife habitat, and it depends on the essential
conditions for any successful business transaction—namely, bringing together willing sellers and able buyers.

In simplified form, The Nature Conservancy identifies land
that it believes needs to be preserved and protected. It then assesses
protection options, including what it would cost to buy the land. If
purchase is the best option, it then goes about raising the money.
There are various ways to accomplish this. Sometimes government
agencies and charitable foundations can be found that will provide the matching funds. Often such agencies will buy the land
from the Conservancy, with covenants and restrictions on its use,
once the first purchase is final. The Nature Conservancy is cau-
tious about taking on the management of all these lands; its purpose is to buy the land or otherwise get it into protected status.

A good example of what The Nature Conservancy does—and
one I know about firsthand, since the Orvis company was involved
—concerned the Henry's Lake outlet, approximately twelve miles
of the Henry's Fork of the Snake's headwater tributaries, which is
important spawning habitat for trout in the upper river. Unfortunately, it was being managed not much differently than an irriga-
tion canal and was completely dry, some years, for months at a time
as water was being stored in anticipation of future agricultural
needs. The fishery was suffering until TNC, with Orvis's help, established a water trust fund and the outright purchase of the Flat
Ranch and four miles of river frontage. This was in 1994, and
today, through water pruchases and other guarantees, TNC and
the irrigators have virtually assured that the river will never again
run dry. The money was important, of course, but the project would
not have been successful if The Nature Conservancy VP for Idaho,
Guy Bonivene, hadn't established a working relationship with the
potato farmers. He was a good old boy who could kick dirt with
the best of them and he got the job done. It took money, organization, and a meeting of the minds, which is a good alternative to
confrontation, regulation, and politics.

There are so many good stories about The Nature Conservancy and the people who make it work. I remember, especially, Nancy MacKinnon, who raised fifteen million dollars to buy and preserve the tall grass prairie in Oklahoma. Her background was Brown University and then San Francisco but she found a way to convince cowboys, Indians, and bankers that the prairie needed saving.

Another example was the way the Conservancy convinced the Florida legislature to enact Proposition 200, which directs $3 billion over ten years to buy and protect critical wildlife habitat. I could go on for many pages about the incredible accomplishments of the TNC staff. The most rewarding work I have done has been with them.

When I first heard of it, The Nature Conservancy was a smaller operation than it is today. Its objectives are now increasingly ambitious, including efforts to protect huge parcels of rain forest, most of them in the hundreds of thousands of acres. The projects run into the millions of dollars and take months or years to conclude. Since my retirement, I have been involved in Conservancy projects of this kind in Belize, Brazil, Indonesia, Mexico, Papua New Guinea, and Paraguay. It has been some of the most satisfying work I've done and has certainly kept me busy. It has also appealed to my sense of optimism. Instead of hand wringing and helplessness in the face of big environmental challenges, The Nature Conservancy is doing something in the most direct way possible. I believe if you can get the right people involved and focused, there are no problems that can't be solved.

In conservation, like in anything else, it is the people who make the thing go, and you find some very dedicated, can-do people who are concerned with helping the environment and preserving what we have. This is especially true of the young people you find working in organizations like The Nature Conservancy.

I have watched them in action and they have come up with some very innovative solutions to tough problems. I particularly remember one case where John Cook of the Conservancy called me and said he needed help. Now, I had a very high regard for John Cook. He had been TNC director for Florida and had done an incredible job handling that state's program, staff, and donors. John had been pulled off that job to handle what were called "special magnum projects." The big ones, in other words. His current magnum project was at Gray Ranch in the southwest corner of New Mexico. It was a five-hundred-square-mile parcel and the Conservancy had committed to buying it. But they needed to find a conservation buyer to sell it to. John had tried Ted Turner and come close. But Ted found another piece of property he liked better.

This made for a problem, because there are not a lot of Ted Turners around who can afford to buy five-hundred-square-mile properties for the sake of conservation. John had a new prospect and he asked me to help convince him to buy Gray Ranch.

"John, I'd be glad to help you," I said, "but tell me how."

He said, "This fellow is a poet and a cowboy and his mission in life is to save the grass range. I need you to convince him that the Conservancy is an outfit he can trust—and to keep up our end on the whiskey drinking. I need to save my liver."

"John," I said, "I think you called the wrong fellow. I don't do poets."

Well, he convinced me and I met with Drum Hadley, his prospect. We hit it off real well. Drum is an extremely bright guy with a great sense of humor and full of fun. My friend and guide from the Keys, Rick Ruoff, joined us on Gray Ranch, where we hunted three kinds of quail that I'd never shot before: scaled quail, Gambel's quail, and Mearns' quail.

The courtship wound up with Drum and his son, Seth, setting up the Animas Foundation to acquire Gray Ranch from the Conservancy, which retained a permanent conservation easement. This led to the development and association of neighboring ranch owners called the Malpai Borderlands Group. The idea was to keep the surrounding ranches in business and protect their open space. This group created something called the "grassbank." To help them revitalize their grasslands and survive the droughts, Drum opened up the Gray for his neighbors' cattle. In return, they signed a conservation easement to never subdivide their home ranches. This was a double conservation win: the Group is well on its way to protecting over a million contiguous acres and the range is being restored to healthy grassland. Today, the Group is working with the neighboring ranches and the public land agencies to restore fire to the country to keep down the woody shrubs like mesquite. This is a great success story of conservation people and cattle people getting together in a win-win situation.

Drum and his son, Seth, by the way, have become good friends. I've made several trips to Gray Ranch and they've visited me at Mays Pond, so I suppose I do poets after all.

I have also served on the board of an organization out in Bozeman, Montana, called PERC—Political, Economic Research Center. This is essentially a think tank with a number of bright, young academics who are trying to promote free-market solutions to environmental problems. Many environmental problems can be solved by private-property owners because property rights have the potential for turning the environment into an asset. For example, PERC promotes purchasing or leasing water rights to increase in-stream flows—this was the answer to the Henry's Fork crisis I just described. PERC has been an important influence on the growing interest in the West in water trading to prevent streams from drying up and killing fish.

I have gotten a lot of satisfaction out of working with PERC (and not just because its annual board meeting is in September when both bird hunting and trout fishing in Montana are superb). Their ideas about free-market solutions to environmental problems match my own experiences. Without question, my best hunting and fishing days have come on private property where landowners have an incentive—either for profit or from personal ethics—to preserve the environment. As we move into the next century, the environmental movement will have to rely more and more on PERC-type solutions if we wish to conserve our precious natural resources.

* * *

When I retired in 1993, Romi and I made Mays Pond Plantation in Monticello, Florida, our permanent residence. I was pleased to be invited to serve on the board of the Tall Timbers Research Station there, since I was familiar with the organization and a firm believer in its goals and objectives. Tall Timbers was originally set up in the 1930s to further the work started by Herbert Stoddard, who was my hero when I was a boy.

Herbert Stoddard was a naturalist, and many believed he knew more about wildlife and what made it tick than anyone alive, in spite of the fact that his formal education ended at the third grade. He was an incredible observer and researcher, and he was not afraid to call things the way he saw them. Stoddard was brought into the Tallahassee area by an association of plantation owners who were concerned about the wildlife populations, especially quail, which were declining. He quickly pointed out that the main reason for this decline was the suppression of fire, which was an article of faith with the U.S. Forest Service and its Smokey the Bear campaign against all woods fires. Stoddard demonstrated that the region of south Georgia and north Florida was a fire ecology area. There are more lightning strikes in Florida than in all other states put together, and Stoddard argued that in the absence of humans and their fire suppression methods 100 percent of the state would burn most years. The plants and animals native to the Red Hills area around Tallahassee had evolved accordingly and actually required fire to maintain their habitat. Old-timers employed what they called controlled burns, setting fire to the woods at the right time of year to consume the fuel that would otherwise feed catastrophic fires. The Forest Service fought this practice until Herbert Stoddard single-handedly convinced it to change its policy, something no government agency does without a lot of resistance.

Stoddard's work so impressed Henry and Edward Beadel, brothers who owned plantations in the Red Hills area, that they decided it should be perpetuated. They left their land and a good part of their estates to the Tall Timbers Research Station, heavily endowing it.

From my experience with Tall Timbers, I learned that such endowments are not always a good thing. The scientists who succeeded Stoddard at Tall Timbers thought that the endowment was all the money they needed and they would play their own game in research, and they as much as told the plantation owners that they didn't need their damn Yankee money. Predictably, this created a rift between Tall Timbers and the plantation owners. The plantations in the Red Hills area consisted of 300,000 acres collectively owned by about fifty families, all of them wealthy and interested in preservation and propagation of wildlife and wildlife habitat.

When I joined the board, Tall Timbers was having trouble living within its budget and was in the process of retaking the organization from the good old boys and getting the plantation community involved again. It wasn't a tough product to sell, and I enjoyed doing it. It was simply a matter of going to the plantation owners and saying, "We need you, and, if you help us, we'll help you reduce your costs and increase your wildlife populations." I went on to convince many plantation owners that it would be very beneficial to put their land into a conservation easement. Ted Turner was the first to put a conservation easement on his plantation. He is a true conservationist and wanted to be sure his land would remain in wildlife habitat in perpetuity, so before Tall Timbers had set up the machinery to handle conservation easements, Ted led the way by giving The Nature Conservancy easements on his plantations in Florida and South Carolina. I followed suit with my land, giving TNC an easement on my plantation. I then became an advocate, selling other plantation owners on the idea of giving easements to the Red Hills subsidiary of Tall Timbers. It wasn't a very tough sell. A conservation easement appeals to the heart because it protects your land from future development and insures that it will forever be wildlife habitat. It also appeals to the pocketbook because you receive a tax deduction. This deduction amounts to the difference in the value of the land with and without the possibility of development and can amount to as much as 40 percent of the value of the land before the easement, and your estate taxes may be reduced. The only negative I can think of is that some future heir, who does not hunt or care passionately about conservation, might not be able to maximize income from the land by developing it. But many of us love our land more than we trust our grandchildren—or our grandchildren-in-law to come.

My work with Tall Timbers has been very rewarding and has given me the pleasure of working for two of my cousins, the Ireland sisters, both Tall Timbers board members—one older and wiser than I; the other, younger and wiser than I. When either Kate Ireland or Louise Humphry calls to tell me what needs to be done, I say, "Yes, ma'am," and I do it. But I have to say, I've never gotten bad instructions from either of these ladies.

I joined the Florida state board of The Nature Conservancy in 1994, when my term on the national board ended. The Conservancy has a good rule—you are elected for three-year terms, but no one, not even officers, can stay more than ten years. The challenges in Florida are certainly big enough to keep anyone busy and engaged. The pressures of development and population growth are a threat to such unique areas as the Everglades, Florida Bay, the Keys and their coral reefs, and the Apalachicola River system. I'm vitally interested in all of these and happy to see both the state and the nation focusing on the problems.

My son Perk succeeded me on The Nature Conservancy national board. At the time, there were two other Orvis board members, Bob Mitchell and Joe Williams, serving on the national board, and Joe was chairman. It was reported to me that some of the other board members were complaining about nepotism when Perk was nominated for a position on the board. I'm told that Bob and Joe spoke up on his behalf, saying in effect, "The kid is smarter and works harder than the old man. This choice has nothing to do with nepotism."

While I already had a pretty full plate in my conservation efforts, in 1995 I agreed to serve on the board of the National Fish and Wildlife Foundation. Orvis had been involved in several joint projects with this organization, and I had a very high regard for the people who ran the NFWF, which had started out administering gifts of property for the benefit of the U.S. Fish and Wildlife Service and then went on to develop creative partnerships with organizations as diverse as the Agency for International Development, the Bureau of Land Management, and the Environmental Protection Agency. My association with the foundation goes back to 1989, when Orvis got involved in a waterfowl project called the North American Waterfowl Management Plan. We matched the first $50,000 in contributions from our customers, which was, in turn, matched by the foundation with its matching federal funds. It sounds very involved but the bottom line was that Orvis effectively doubled the funds available to NAWMP at the time when waterfowl needed all the help they could get. Since then, Orvis and its customers have contributed almost $800,000 to National Fish and Wildlife Foundation projects ranging from Kodiak Island in Alaska to Florida Bay.

Another organization I've worked for, though not as a board member, is Coastal Conservation of Florida. This is an extremely effective organization that accomplishes a great deal with a very small budget. In the few years that I've been helping them, they've succeeded in getting redfish classified as a game fish, which eliminated commercial fishing for redfish; establishing a saltwater fishing license for the state of Florida; and, most important, banning commercial netting operations within three miles of shore. This ban has had a tremendously positive effect on the populations of sea trout, redfish, and especially mullet, which is the main food source for many of our game fish. The fight to ban nets was very tough, but the results have been more than worth it.

In the course of working on these various projects in Florida, I met with the late governor Lawton Chiles. We did some quail hunting together on my place, and I found him to be not only an engaging personality but also someone deeply committed to conservation. Lawton would have joined the Tall Timbers board in March of 1999 after he retired as governor, but he died of a heart attack in December 1998.

As encouraging as it is to have such people at the top, that isn't as important as what happens out in the field—and in the rivers and streams. I am proud of what we have done as a family and through the Orvis company, and I am terrifically encouraged by the prospects for the future. The last twenty or thirty years have been great for the cause of conservation. Once in a while, you hear grumbling about how bad things are and how it isn't like it was in the good old days. The people who say these things have selective memories, limited experience, or both.

I tell people every day that for an American sportsman, these *are* the good old days. The preservation of habitat, the wise management of resources, and the work of organizations like the ones I've mentioned have resulted in great comebacks for game and fish species and created wonderful opportunities for sportsmen. There are all sorts of examples of this. When I was a kid, if you saw a white-tailed deer in the woods, that was a very big occasion. Now, as everybody knows, deer are so abundant they are considered pests in many areas. The deer season in Florida is seventy days long, and the limit is three bucks a day, with special doe days. And even with that liberal limit, there is no shortage of deer.

Another example is the wild turkey, which I hunted as a boy in Florida, but which had virtually disappeared from most of its former range. There weren't any turkeys in Vermont when I moved there in 1965. Wildlife managers trapped thirty-one wild turkeys in western New York State and released them in Vermont in 1969, a few miles from the Orvis headquarters. Today, there is a thriving population of turkeys in Vermont and a hunting season that lasts the entire month of May. That, combined with the Hendrickson and Red Quill hatch on the Battenkill, makes May one of my favorite months.

Duck populations have also made a fantastic rebound over the last three years, far beyond the most hopeful expectations of concerned duck hunters. When I was a boy and first started shooting ducks, the limit was twelve, but no wood ducks were permitted. Today, the beautiful wood duck is our most common duck in Vermont and Florida. I've seen as many as fifteen hundred wood ducks come into a thirty-acre pond in one evening.

In the world of angling, the news is just as good if not better. The catch-and-release message has sunk in, and many streams in the East that were once just put-and-take—with not very challenging, hatchery-raised fish being caught before they'd spent even a full night in the river—now support healthy populations of wild trout. More and more, a big increase in angling pressure has meant not that fishing has declined but that anglers' views are being considered, and are prevailing, in fights over how to manage water resources. Consequently, we have learned how to do many things better and have brought back some streams— especially spring creeks—that had been destroyed or brought way down in quality.

My old friend Vern Bressler did this on some property I bought in Wyoming. Grazing cattle had trampled the spring creeks on this land into wide, shallow wallows that were useless as trout habitat. Vern rebuilt the banks to narrow the streams back down to their previous size, and generally restored them to their condition before the cattle had taken over. In a couple of seasons, we were catching (and releasing) brown, rainbow, and cutthroat trout—some of them twenty-four inches long—from these little streams.

So many things have gotten better in so many ways. Thousands of people have gotten very involved in conservation, and a lot of them have put their money where their interests are. That combination of money and commitment has accomplished a lot in the way of fish and wildlife conservation through good science and hard work, all of which means that these truly are the good old days.

This couldn't suit me better. While I have devoted a lot of time and energy in my retirement to working for conservationist causes, I have plenty of time left over to do the things I like doing most— fishing and hunting. When I first retired, someone said to Romi that I would now have more time for fishing and hunting. She replied that it would be impossible for me to do any more.

Well, I quickly proved her wrong. In my last year as CEO of Orvis, I managed 168 days in the field—no doubt spending part of some of those days in the office. Since I've retired, the best I've been able to manage is 277 days in a single year. The worst is 255.

Even with all this time on my hands, I still can't fit everything in. Sometimes I can't figure out how I ever had time to work. There are so many things I've done and want to do again—as well as so many things that I haven't done and would like to try. But for me, there just aren't enough days in the year, even when you are in the field for three quarters of them.

In January, I'll be at my place in Florida, where I hunt quail —plantation style from a mule wagon or off horseback with my dogs—and go duck hunting with my old Lab, Bernie. The plantation life is especially good for a grandfather because there is so much that the grandchildren like doing there that I get to do with them. The quail hunting ends in early March. In the second week of March, Romi and I go up into the Everglades, one of our favorite places, on a trawler that is owned by a friend named Rick Cappeletti, who is a retired policeman from Miami. Another friend, Rick Ruoff, who is one of the finest guides in the Keys, brings his flats skiff, which we use to get around and fish for tarpon, redfish, and snook. Ruoff allows us to kill one fish a trip, and there is nothing better than grilled snook over buttonwood coals. We have been doing this for a long time, and we still find the Everglades, with all its bird life, a magical place. Sometimes we don't see another soul for two days.

Spring turkey season starts in Florida and Georgia the third week of March, and I rarely miss a morning. I average about one turkey every ten mornings. This is truly hunting, not shooting—

no dogs involved. But being in the deep woods when wildlife wakes up before dawn is a true delight in the early spring. There are new migrating birds and new emerging wildflowers each morning. I will usually have a conversation with a gobbler as we call back and forth across the woods—even if I don't convince him that I am attractive enough to visit. Afternoons and evenings are great for fly-rodding for bass and blue gill, and the woods are full of dogwood, redbud, plum blossoms, and yellow jasmine.

About every other year we will go to Argentina the second week of April to fish for trout and then open the duck season there. At the end of April, we will return to Vermont to enjoy spring all over again. Turkey season starts May first, and this coincides with the spring migration of warblers and thrushes, the oriole and the rose-breasted grosbeak. There are also fiddlehead ferns and morel mushrooms to pick. Best of all, the Hendricksons hatch on the Battenkill at about 2:30 every afternoon, and they are followed a week later by the Red Quill spinner fall in the evening.

In early June, we will go down to the Keys for tarpon and bonefish, with the Ricks, Ruoff and Cappeletti. This is a trip I like an awful lot. We use the trawler as a mother ship and fish the Marquesas, a beautiful atoll off Key West. This is a good place to catch the big three of saltwater fly-fishing—bonefish, permit, and tarpon. I've caught every combination of two in a day but never all three.

Later in June, we travel to England, where we sometimes have an Orvis board meeting and fish the classic chalk streams— the Test and the Itchen—for trout.

In early July, Romi and I are often guests at two salmon camps in Canada—one on the Upsalquich River in New Brunswick and the other on the Grand Cascapedia in Quebec. Mid-July finds us in Wyoming at our log cabin, which Romi had built on a spring creek.

We have another Orvis board meeting in August in Wyoming, and our directors have a chance to fish for sighted big trout in crystal clear water with tiny flies or take an overnight float trip on the

South Fork of the Snake River in Idaho, where there is superb cutthroat fishing and a beautiful canyon with bald and golden eagles.

September is when bird season opens out west. I meander through central and eastern Montana, hunting sharptail, huns, and sage grouse. By the end of September, I have joined a friend in southwest Idaho for chukar and quail hunting. We also catch the opening of grouse hunting in Wyoming, where I hunt blue, sage, and ruffed grouse. Duck season in Wyoming opens on the first Saturday in October, and we have two or three days of excellent mallard and teal shooting on our spring creeks.

October finds me in Vermont, and by this time I have walked myself into pretty good shape for grouse and woodcock in the tough, sidehill coverts of New England.

Orvis has its annual stockholders meeting in Cleveland the second week of November. Two of our directors, Dick Whitney and Al Whitehouse, invite the rest of the board to shoot ducks at one of the oldest duck clubs in the country, located on Lake Erie. By the middle of November, we are back in Florida to open the quail and duck seasons there and looking forward to having the children and grandchildren for Thanksgiving and Christmas.

Sport keeps me busy, and it never seems to get old. The feeling for the game is still there, just as strong as it ever was. I couldn't imagine not feeling excited when ducks are decoying, or my fly is drifting over the spot where I've just seen a trout rise, or when a dog suddenly goes on point. I'm not as interested in the numbers or in keeping score as I was when I started—just being there is the thing.

I've been lucky enough to build a life and a successful business around what has meant so much to me and has given me so much satisfaction—and still do. I am also proud to have built a successful business in a dynamic industry and to have used my success to give something back—in the form of my conservation efforts. I feel fortunate to have had the opportunity to do all this and to have had a hell of a good time along the way. I believe I can safely say, as I did to that *Wall Street Journal* reporter some years back, that I never gave anyone a reason to feel sorry for me. That's not a bad record for a kid whose mother thought he might grow up and make a good dog handler some day. Then again, I might have been just as happy being a damn good dog trainer.

A History of Leigh Perkins at Orvis

A parody of the time line of the history of Orvis since it was acquired by Leigh, created in honor of his retirement.

The Official History		The Real Story . . .

Leigh H. Perkins buys the Orvis Company with annual sales of $500,000.

← **1965** →

LHP passes up an opportunity to purchase a company that makes falsies.

America's first fly fishing school opens at Orvis Manchester.

← **1966** →

In true Perkins fashion, LHP flies in the face of conventional supply and demand economics by *creating* demand.

Orvis offers world's first "Zinger" (pin-on reel).

← **1967** →

First saw the Zinger pinned on the chest of a busty waitress.

1969 →

Indicted (and acquitted) by justice department for doing commerce with communist China.

Orvis is first to produce and market Georgia Fatwood.

← **1972** →

Pinky gets his first job.

LHP perfects duck soup recipe.

← **1973** →

LHP writes "Game Cookery" on a flight from New Zealand in hopes of boosting sales of a $300 thermometer.

Orvis opens America's first dedicated wingshooting school in Manchester.

← **1973** →

Results in LHP getting sued for causing a neighbor to become impotent.

SALES REACH $5 MILLION ANNUALLY	← **1973** →	LHP claims he'll buy a company plane if sales ever reach $10 million.

Orvis introduces first graphite rods. ← **1974** →

LHP would like to say the move to graphite was visionary, but actually he was running out of bamboo.

Orvis introduces Dog's Nest® to America.

← **1977** →

First sample of Dog's Nest given as gift for gin-drinking goat named "Williams."

Orvis establishes mail order and retail business in England. 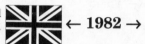 ← **1982** →

Brits are overheard saying, "Now we'll have all the damn Yanks running up and down the banks."

 Orvis-Endorsed Lodges, Outfitters, and Guides Program is created, defining standards of quality and responsibility. ← **1986** →

This program was actually established to ensure LHP a constant source of spunky fly fishing and shooting pals to bum around with worldwide.

SALES REACH $50 MILLION ANNUALLY	← **1986** →	Still no plane . . .

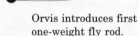

Orvis introduces first one-weight fly rod. ← **1987** →

One problem—no line manufacturer makes one-weight line.

 Orvis fly rods named #1 best-made products of the 1980s by Tom Peters, author of *In Search of Excellence.* ← **1989** →

LHP decides maybe business soothsayers aren't all b.s.

SALES REACH $100 MILLION ANNUALLY	← **1993** →	Still no plane . . . Credibility on this begins to wane.